healthy Indian in minutes

Monisha Bharadwaj

healthy Indian
in minutes

fast food, fabulous flavours

with photographs by Georgia Glynn Smith

KYLE CATHIE LIMITED

This book is for the most wonderful children in the world, Arrush and India Saayli.

acknowledgements

Another big thank you to Kyle Cathie and her fabulous team, who create such wonderful books out of my words. A *namaste* to Catherine Ward, my editor, who asked all the right questions to refine the book, and to my family who brought me up with an instinctive knowledge of what to eat and when.

Editor Catherine Ward
Design by Mark Latter www.pinkstripedesign.com
Photography by Georgia Glynn Smith
Assistant Sue Prescot
Home economy by Valerie Berry
Assistants Fern Green & Mima Sinclair
Repro by Colourscan
Printed and bound by Craftprint

First printed in Great Britain in 2009 by
Kyle Cathie Limited
122 Arlington Road
London NW1 7HP
general.enquiries@kyle-cathie.com
www.kylecathie.com

ISBN 978 1 85626 848 6

contents

introduction

We all know that what we choose to eat influences our health, our energy levels and our well-being. There is more and more awareness about what is good for us and we know that we should be eating more fruit and vegetables, fibre and unprocessed foods. Bad eating habits only exacerbate today's stressful lifestyle and we can no longer afford to disregard the ill effects they have on us.

a gentle cuisine

Although many people outside India believe that Indian food is greasy and spicy, everyday Indian home cooking is not unhealthy or fattening. In fact, it is a highly nutritious, gentle cuisine that has always included natural and whole foods such as wholewheat flour, raw cane sugar, lots of vegetables, beans, lentils and any number of healing spices. Food found in takeaways and restaurants is much greasier and spicier than what people traditionally eat at home and, contrary to the belief that it's quicker to order a takeaway, I believe that my recipes are generally faster as well as healthier and fresher in taste.

seasonal ingredients

In the West, it is possible to buy most foods all year round. However, in India many people's diets are dictated by what is available according to the season. India's national fruit, the mango, for example, is only available for a few months each year. I remember how, when I was growing up in Mumbai, we would wait for the first Alphonso mangoes to come into the market in April. Eating the first mango of the year was quite an occasion and an endless amount would be consumed over the ensuing summer months. The first rains in June, however, would finish the Alphonso crop and then we would have the 'monsoon' varieties to look forward to, such as Totapuri and Langda. We would have to wait a whole year to eat Alphonso mangoes again!

Traditionally, people in India have bought only local food. Even today, farmers take their produce to the nearest market and sell everything before going home at night. Many people buy only what they need for the day, so a trip to the market to buy the freshest ingredients is a daily ritual.

a diverse cuisine

The greatest strength of Indian cooking has been its ability to absorb outside influences wholeheartedly and make them a part of native eating habits. The term 'Indian cooking' is often considered too generic because it does not take into the account the great diversity that exists within the cuisine. What most people around the world see as Indian food is often northern Indian cooking, although this is slowly changing in some countries. This is, perhaps, why the term 'authentic' does not seem to apply to Indian cooking. What is really authentic in an ancient cuisine that has been influenced by so many cultures? The samosa, which is now so quintessentially Indian, was introduced to India by the Mughals. Chillies and potatoes were brought by the Portuguese. Today, Indians grow mushrooms, avocados and baby corn for export and all these have found their way into Indian cooking.

AYURVEDA

The basis of all Indian cookery is the ancient science of Ayurveda. Ayurveda, the Indian system of holistic healing, is the oldest form of medicine known to man. It was written down about 5,000 years ago by Himalayan sages who understood the value and health effects of the various herbs that grew around them.

Ayurveda believes that we can achieve optimum health by nourishing the 'dhatus' or the seven major kinds of tissues, including the muscles, fat and bony tissue, and by cleansing the body of 'ama' or the toxic waste that accumulates due to poor digestion or wrong absorption. These days, ama will also include the ill effects of pollution.

The Indian kitchen is an apothecary that tends to the everyday health and well-being needs of the family. The food that is prepared daily must be fresh, must use healing spices and herbs and has to include a host of food groups to make it complete. A traditional Indian meal must be balanced and consists of a carbohydrate, a protein-rich curry, fruit, vegetables, and dairy in the form of yogurt, cheese or milk (see page 15 for more on this).

the three 'doshas'

Ayurveda refers to the unique combination of energy present in every person at birth as that person's constitution or 'dosha'.

The three doshas are Vata (governed by space and air), Pitta (governed by fire and water) and Kapha (governed by water and earth). If we recognise the needs of our own constitution and choose our food and lifestyle accordingly, we have a better chance of achieving good health. No two people are alike and each of us will respond to foods in a unique way. Often two doshas can be present in person at the same time, or doshas might change according to the season. At times, all the doshas combine in an individual, making the constitution a balanced or 'tridoshic' one.

satmya and okasatmya

The Ayurvedic concept of 'satmya' refers to anything that is beneficial to the body and mind, even long after you have eaten it. 'Okasatmya', on the other hand, is when a particular diet or lifestyle has become non-harmful to the body through regular use. Some nations, for example, eat vast amounts of cheese and most people from that country are able to digest it easily. However, if a person from a country that does not eat a lot of cheese suddenly begins to eat it every day, it is almost certain that he or she will not be able to metabolise it as well as the regular cheese eaters. Given your constitution and ancestry, something that works well for you may be disastrous for another person.

VATA

Vata is governed by the elements of space and air. It is described as dry, rough, restless and light. Recipes that are suitable for Vata carry a cloud symbol.

Vata characteristics

You know that you have a Vata constitution if you are lean and possibly too tall or too short. You find it difficult to put on weight. Your skin is dry and sensitive with a tendency towards dullness and wrinkles, your hair is rough and kinky and your hands and feet are often cold. You suffer from constipation, brittle nails and perspire little. You prefer a warm, sunny climate, have a variable appetite, dislike routine and love to be physically active. You dream often (of flying, moving or jumping), but do not remember your dreams. You find yourself snacking often and you sleep light. When stressed, you veer towards fear or anxiety.

Vata imbalance

Sometimes the Vata dosha may increase, leading to imbalances in health. Eating too many dry or raw foods, inadequate sleep, too much travel and therefore changes in your routine, too many very cold drinks and exposure to cold winds might be the cause.

You will know that your Vata has increased if:
- your skin is feeling tight and dry
- your hair is drier, with a tendency towards split ends
- you are anxious, worried or moody
- you feel more restless than usual
- your throat feels dry and your lips are chapped
- your digestion becomes irregular and you have flatulence
- you find it difficult to fall asleep

Vata is dry, rough, cool and constantly moving. Staying warm and establishing a regular routine should bring your dosha back into balance. Try the following:

- Create a regular routine, which includes going to bed and waking up at the same time each day, eating three proper meals at the right time and working and resting regularly.

- Bring your power of digestion or 'agni' back into balance by eating a light breakfast, a nourishing lunch and a light dinner. Sit down to eat, concentrate on your food and don't rush through it. Allow a few minutes rest after you have eaten.

- Give yourself an oil massage every day. Rub some almond or olive oil into your skin and pamper yourself by kneading and stroking. If you plan to wash your hair, rub some oil into your scalp as well. Allow it to soak into your scalp and wash off after an hour.

- Protect yourself from the cold. It is better to be warm than freezing, so cover your ears, hands and feet and apply lip balm to chapped lips.

- Walk for 30 minutes each day – this is the best exercise for Vata.

- Switch off completely before you go to sleep. Turn off all stimulants such as the TV or radio, read a soothing book, have a glass of warm milk and wear comfortable night clothes.

The Ayurvedic tastes that help balance Vata are sour, salty and sweet, so include more of these in your diet – try foods such as citrus fruits, nuts, dried fruit and beans (see page 12). Look out for the cloud symbol alongside the recipes.

PITTA

Pitta is governed by the elements of fire and water. It is described as hot, acidic, sharp and burning. Recipes that are suitable for Pitta carry a flame symbol.

Pitta characteristics

A Pitta person is generally of medium build and well-proportioned. You lose or gain weight easily and have a good appetite and metabolism. You therefore require frequent meals and are rarely constipated. Your hair and skin are oily and fine and you are prone to spots and rashes. Creative and competitive, you are also intellectual and have strong opinions. You become angry and frustrated when stressed and are vehement about putting across your point of view. You perspire freely, your hands are warm and you are frequently thirsty.

Pitta imbalance

Sometimes Pitta becomes imbalanced due to factors such as eating too many hot and spicy foods, lack of sleep, hot weather, overexposure to the sun or skipping meals.

You will know that your Pitta has increased if:
- you have heartburn and feel acidic
- your skin feels hot and burned
- you start to lose more hair than usual
- you feel temperamental, angry and less tolerant of others
- your sleep becomes irregular
- you become overly obsessed with work

Pitta is hot. Staying cool, both physically and emotionally, will help bring your dosha back into balance. Try the following:

- Avoid spicy foods. Snack on sweet fruits, such as grapes and pears. Eat at regular mealtimes to avoid acidity.

- Avoid going out in the sun when it is at its hottest. This aggravates Pitta and leaves you feeing burned inside and out. Protect yourself with a hat, sunglasses and cotton or linen clothing.

- Drink plenty of water at room temperature, eat fruit and vegetables and try to make a habit of it. Daily elimination is essential to avoid a build-up of toxic waste.

- Take things in your stride emotionally. If you find that a situation aggravates you, step away from it. Try meditation, long, leisurely walks and find harmony with nature.

- Go swimming to help you cool down.

- Nourish your skin with moisturisers and massages. Rub massage oil into your skin to cool and polish it.

The Ayurvedic tastes that balance Pitta are sweet, astringent and bitter – milk, rice, fruit and nuts are all beneficial (see page 12). Look out for the flame symbol alongside the recipes.

KAPHA

Kapha is governed by the elements of water and earth. It is described as heavy, cold, slippery and sweet. Recipes that are suitable for Kapha carry a raindrop symbol.

Kapha characteristics

Robust in build, you have heavy bones and gain weight easily, but find it difficult to lose it. Your skin is thick and cool and you are prone to clogged pores and spots. Your hair is thick and wavy. You prefer a dry climate and are comfortable in hot or cold weather. Regular bowel movements, a good appetite, and a normal digestion are not affected by your love of fatty, starchy foods. You love leisure activities, sleep soundly and often dream of water and rivers. Your opinions and ideas are slow to change and you tend to avoid difficult situations. When you are ill, you tend to retain fluid or produce a lot of mucus.

Kapha imbalance

Kapha can become imbalanced due to too many cold foods or drinks, a lack of exercise, lack of sleep and a heavy diet of fried, sweet or processed foods.

You will know that your Kapha has increased if:
- your nose and throat feel heavy and congested when you wake up
- you have a runny nose throughout the day
- your digestion is slow and elimination is irregular
- you feel sluggish and dull
- your hair and skin are oilier than usual
- you feel like being on the outside, looking in at the world, rather than participating

Kapha is heavy and cold. Keeping fit and warm will bring your dosha back into balance. Try the following:

- Exercise is the first step to balancing Kapha. This dosha needs both physical and mental activity. Find a form of exercise that is rigorous without being exhausting, as well as mental challenges such as learning a new skill or doing puzzles and crosswords.

- Eat regular meals to kick-start the digestion.

- As your digestion can become sluggish, you need to eat foods such as fruits, dry foods such as cereals and light foods such as soups.

- Do not expose yourself to the cold and drink plenty of warm water.

- Try to maintain a regular bedtime routine. Sleep early and wake up early.

- Create new experiences for yourself – meet new people, travel, organise an event.

The Ayurvedic tastes that balance Kapha are bitter, pungent and astringent (see page 12). Choose foods such as couscous, cabbage, okra and ginger. Rice and wheat are heavy and should be eaten in moderation. Look for the raindrop symbol alongside the recipes.

AYURVEDIC NUTRITION

According to Ayurveda, all foods consist of six tastes or 'rasas', two potencies or 'viryas' and three post-digestive, long-term effects on the body or 'vipaks'.

creating a balanced meal

The word 'rasa' has many meanings in Sanskrit and other Indian languages. It can mean taste as well as emotion and is an important concept in Indian cookery. I have always believed that for an Indian meal to be successful, it must have a balance of all the six tastes, and this is what I have tried to achieve in my menu plans. Sweetness may come through onions or certain spices; heat does not have to come in the form of chillies, but can come from ginger and garlic as well; astringency might be supplied in the form of a cleansing salad or raita.

THE SIX RASAS

For an Indian meal to be successful, it is important to include all of the six tastes or 'rasas'.

sweet

This taste has a cooling potency and tends to be heavy and moist. In moderation, it has a satisfying quality and emotionally it promotes a feeling of well-being. Sweet ingredients include onions, tomatoes, cardamom and prawns.

sour

The potency of sour is heating and therefore this taste boosts the digestion. It can be mildly heavy and moist. Sour ingredients include lemons, oranges, tamarind *(below left)* and vinegar.

salty

This taste has the qualities of water and fire, which gives it its heating potency. Its long-term effect is moistening and therefore people who eat too much salt are prone to water retention.

spicy hot

This taste is most stimulating to the digestion. Its qualities are light and dry. Spicy, hot ingredients include ginger, garlic, chillies, pepper and cloves.

bitter

Bitter tastes are cold, dry and light. They balance the other tastes and are a vital taste for overall health. Bitter ingredients include cumin, fenugreek, mustard seeds and bitter gourd ('karela').

astringent

This taste is slightly light and dry with a cooling potency. Astringent ingredients slow the digestion and create an emotional sense of detachment. Astringent ingredients include tea, pomegranates and aubergines *(opposite)*.

EIGHT RULES OF AN AYURVEDIC DIET

prakruti

Choose a combination of foods depending on their nature – meat is heavy to digest, vegetables are light. If you choose all heavy ingredients in a single meal, you will feel bloated and the food will not be properly digested.

karana

Consider how you process your food. In general, cooked foods are easier to digest with the exception of fruits and some vegetables such as carrots. Frying adds heaviness; stir-frying helps introduce lightness. Microwave cooking destroys the life force of a food, which is called 'prana'.

samyoga

Never mix contrary foods. For example, fish and some dairy are not combined because they both need a different rate of acid secretion, as well as concentration of acid for proper digestion. Bananas and milk do not go well together either.

rashi

Control the quantity of food you eat according to your constitution.

desha

Eat according to your environment. Consider the seasons, and factors such as pollution.

kala

Be attentive to the time of eating. Eat only when the previous meal has been properly digested.

upayoga sanstha

Follow the rules of eating. Eat food when it is hot. Focus on eating, rather than on laughing, talking or reading. Be calm and unhurried; drinking too much during a meal or smoking is not advisable.

upabhokta

Every person must decide on what to eat depending on how he or she feels. Never force yourself to eat against your instinct.

THE VIRYAS

Ayurveda refers to the body's power to digest foods as its digestive fire or 'agni'. Consuming too much food, or lots of foods that are cooling, heavy or contaminated, rapidly puts out this fire; too little food does not kindle it enough.

All foods have a heating or cooling effect on the body, known as a 'virya'. Most children in India are taught about heating and cooling foods and how they affect the body during the various seasons. Summers are meant for cooling foods such as milk, coconut and fennel. Winters are for warming foods such as honey, sesame and warming spices such as cloves.

As a child, I was always made to understand the need to eat according to the seasons. This did not simply mean eating seasonal foods, but also understanding how different foods affect the body through the seasons. In summer, if you ate too many mangoes, which are hot, you then had to balance them with a glass of cooling milk!

HEALTHY COOKING TECHNIQUES AND BASIC EQUIPMENT

Much of the so-called Indian takeaway food we are familiar with in the West is considered to be greasy, fattening and unhealthy – not something to be consumed on a regular basis! And yet, Indian home cooking is actually prepared using very healthy techniques.

stir-frying

Stir-frying (rather than deep-frying) is a quick method of cooking using minimal oil – most of my recipes use 1–2 tablespoons vegetable oil. This is heated to a high temperature to stop it from saturating the food, and the ingredients are cooked rapidly over a high heat to preserve their goodness. None of the recipes is deep-fried – even the samosas are oven baked.

sprouting

Sprouting of legumes makes them healthier and higher in vitamins. I regularly sprout green mung beans, brown lentils and moth beans. Simply place the beans in a bowl, cover them with water and soak them overnight to soften their skins. The following morning, tie them up in a tea towel and put them in a warm place to sprout for 1–3 days. If the weather is very hot, I simply drain them and leave them out in the kitchen in a colander or sieve.

fermenting

Another method used to make foods healthier is fermentation. This process applies not only to yogurt, but also to batters such as the one used to make 'dosas' or southern Indian pancakes. Fermentation produces organic acids, which help preserve the food as well as increasing nutritional values.

pressure cooking

I am a great advocate of pressure cooking. It is a method of cooking that is extremely popular in India and, at a time when we are all thinking about the environment, it saves on gas as well. From a health point of view, the nutrients in the food are preserved because they are cooked in steam. Although pressure cooking has become unfashionable in the last few years, to me it is one of the fastest, more environmentally friendly, healthy ways of cooking.

equipment

The average Western kitchen should have all the equipment necessary for the recipes in this book. Most Indian dishes are prepared in one pot, with several processes following on from one another – saving on the washing up!

I recommend using heavy-based pans because they retain and transfer heat better, and they can be heated to higher temperatures. Most Indian cooks use a heavy-based 'kadhai' for stir-frying and deep-frying; this is similar in shape to a Chinese wok but heavier because the food is cooked for longer periods of time.

Another important piece of equipment is an upright blender for making curry pastes and chutneys. I use a large blender for big quantities and a small coffee mill for spice powders.

HOW TO USE THIS BOOK

I have divided the chapters in this book according to how an Indian meal is composed. To begin with, choose a carbohydrate from the first chapter. This becomes the substance of the meal. Then add a curry – meat, chicken, fish or seafood, lentil, bean, vegetable or egg. This provides the moisture and, often, the protein.
Next, choose a 'dry' vegetable accompaniment from the Vegetable Side Dishes chapter. This provides additional nutrition, including fibre. You can then select a salad or relish to complement the meal. Most everyday meals consist of 3–4 dishes and they are always accompanied by water. To help you select dishes that go well together, look out for the menu plans throughout the book – there is something for every budget and occasion, from a healthy packed lunch to take to the office (page 132) to an Indian Sunday brunch (page 100) or a full-blown Diwali feast (page 127). If you're short of time, turn to the All-in-one Meals and Light Snacks chapter on page 118.

quantities

All the recipes in this book serve four people. If you wish to make only enough for two, you will need to reduce the main ingredient down by half but reduce the spices only slightly. Similarly, to increase the portion sizes, increase the spice quantities only slightly. Doubling them will make the dish too intense.

salt

I have not given any measures for salt in my recipes. People differ in their need for salt – some do not eat it at all! Do use your judgement when adding salt to the recipes – my own belief is that there should be enough salt to bring out the other flavours in the dish, but not so much that you need to drink water all through the meal.

experimentation

My recipes try to bring about a balance of flavours so that the food is neither too hot, nor too salty. I tend to be conservative in my use of chillies and chilli powder because I do not like my food overwhelmed by spice and heat. If you prefer a hotter experience, either alter the levels of chilli in the dish, or add a burst of heat with a commercially-bought pickle. A range of pickles and chutneys – from hot chilli or lime to sweet mango or papaya – is served with every meal in India so that each person can design their own level of heat.

Although all the recipes in this book have been measured and tested, I believe that the best cooks use a big dose of intuition and judgement. I have found during many years of teaching and demonstrating that however accurate an ingredients list may be, different people use different ingredients based on what is available. Do touch and smell your ingredients, both as they cook and when they are ready. They will provide you with the best possible clues about how the dish is likely to turn out.

nutrition and your body

Although I have listed the health benefits of many foods alongside the recipes, how they will affect you individually will depend on how your body responds to them. After all, Ayurvedic nutrition is all about eating what makes you, personally, feel healthy and contented – and because this can change with the seasons or years, it is an ongoing process of discovery.

disclaimer

The information and recipes in this book are not intended to diagnose, treat or cure. The book is not a substitute for professional medical advice. If in doubt, please consult your doctor.

one
rice dishes
and bread

An Indian meal is based around the main carbohydrate dish. Most people in India eat rice or wheat every day and both are grown extensively. India was one of the earliest countries to grow rice. From here it travelled first to Egypt, then via Greece, Portugal and Italy to America.

Although India grows hundreds of varieties of rice, basmati is most popular the world over. Its name is associated with visions of lush, green paddy fields being watered by the snow-fed rivers of the Himalayas. Basmati is considered to be the king of rice and, as such, in India it is reserved for special occasions or particular dishes. Like wine, rice gets better with age. Premium basmati rice is left to mature in controlled conditions for up to 10 years, resulting in a rice that cooks better and remains fluffy. New rice is used mainly in puddings because of its sticky texture.

Wheat is a popular grain in India, but more so in the north than in the south. It is made into a whole variety of breads and eaten for breakfast, as a snack or as a main meal. There are also a host of other grains for making bread – including millet ('bajra') and maize or corn – and a large number of products made out of rice and wheat such as rice flour or semolina.

Ayurvedic wisdom

All grains have a sweet 'rasa' or taste. This means that when we eat them they produce a feeling of calmness and satisfaction. While brown rice is favoured in the West for its high fibre and nutrient content, Ayurveda recommends white basmati rice which is lighter and easier to digest. White rice is the only grain that is 'tridoshic' – that is, suitable for all the constitutions (see page 8).

CHAVAL 🐘 🔥

plain boiled rice

In India, people buy rice from their local grocer who has sacks of all the different varieties on display. The older the rice, the fluffier it will be when cooked. New rice is stickier in texture, making it more suitable for puddings and pancakes. It is impossible to tell the age of rice when it comes packed in a bag, but most of the well-known brands I have used in the West work well with the cooking time I have suggested.

200g basmati rice
400ml hot water

preparation time 5 minutes
cooking time 20 minutes
serves 4

1. First wash the rice by placing it in a sieve under cold, running water. Put the drained rice in a heavy-based saucepan with the hot water and bring to the boil – no need to add salt.

2. Reduce the heat, stir and cover with a lid. Simmer for 10 minutes until the rice is fluffy and cooked and the water has been absorbed. Turn off the heat and leave the pan, covered, for a further 5 minutes so that the rice softens in the steam.

3. Open the pan and gently run a fork through the rice to loosen it. Serve hot.

TOMATOCHI LAPSI

broken wheat flavoured with tomato

Broken wheat is wheat that has been ground into smaller bits to make it easy to cook. It is fairly popular in India as a substitute for rice in restricted diets, especially for people who suffer from diabetes, and is also eaten by Hindus as a sweet porridge on religious days. Broken wheat is high in dietary fibre and manganese.

2 tablespoons tomato purée
½ teaspoon garam masala
½ teaspoon turmeric powder
salt, to taste
600ml water
300g broken wheat, washed and drained

preparation time 5 minutes
cooking time 25 minutes
serves 4

1. Combine the tomato purée, spice powders, salt and water in a saucepan and bring to the boil.

2. Add the broken wheat and bring back to the boil. Reduce the heat, cover with a lid and simmer for 10–12 minutes until the wheat is soft. The texture will remain a little chewy because of the nature of the grain.

3. Fluff the wheat with a fork and serve with a lentil dish and side salad.

---

an easy dinner for new cooks

- broken wheat flavoured with tomato (TOMATOCHI LAPSI)
- minced lamb with mushrooms and peas (KHEEMA GUCCHI MUTTER), page 40
- cucumber and mint raita (KHEERE PUDINA KA RAITA), page 136

RATAN KOFTA PULAO 🌸 🔥

jewelled rice with meatballs

I love this festive rice dish that is so simple to make – and so do my children. You can experiment with other vegetables if you prefer – mushrooms, aubergines or or broccoli. Serve with a simple, green salad drizzled with lemon juice.

150g lean minced lamb
1 teaspoon ginger-garlic paste
   (see page 173)
salt, to taste
1 tablespoon sunflower oil
1 teaspoon cumin seeds
150g diced mixed vegetables (e.g.
   carrot, peas, sweetcorn and
   green beans)
½ teaspoon turmeric powder
½ teaspoon garam masala
300g basmati rice, washed
   and drained
600ml water
small handful fresh
   coriander leaves, washed

preparation time 10 minutes
cooking time 30 minutes
serves 4

1. Preheat your oven to 200°C/400°F/gas mark 5. Combine the minced lamb with the ginger-garlic paste and salt and knead well. Shape into little balls each the size of a cherry – I normally get 18 out of this quantity – and place on a non-stick baking tray. Bake in the preheated oven for 15 minutes.

2. Meanwhile, heat the oil in a large, heavy-based saucepan and fry the cumin seeds for a few seconds until they start to darken. Add the mixed vegetables, turmeric and garam masala and give everything a quick stir to coat the vegetables in the oil and spices.

3. Add the rice along with 600ml water. Bring to the boil, stir once, and then reduce the heat to minimum, cover with a lid and simmer for 10 minutes.

4. Turn off the heat and let the rice stand, covered, for 5 minutes. Remove the meatballs from the oven.

5. To serve, fluff up the rice with a fork, dot with the meatballs and drizzle with any of the cooking juices from the baking tray. Garnish with fresh coriander.

GAJAR KI KHICHADI

rice, carrot and lentil stew

A 'khichadi' is a combination of rice and split mung dal, cooked together until creamy – not unlike a risotto. Khichadis are easy to digest and they are therefore always included in a cleansing Ayurvedic diet.

Regarding using whole spices, I dislike biting into them in recipes such as this one, so I prefer to put the spices into a tea infuser (a small gadget that looks like a mesh ball) and place the infuser in the cooking pot. At the end of cooking, I simply take out the infuser and discard the spices. If you don't have a tea infuser, simply tie the spices in a scrap of clean cloth.

1 tablespoon sunflower oil
½ teaspoon cumin seeds
300g white basmati rice,
   washed and drained
4 tablespoons split mung dal,
   washed and drained
2 small carrots, washed and
   roughly grated
5 cloves, 10 peppercorns and 1 bay
   leaf, all placed in a tea infuser
900ml water
½ teaspoon turmeric powder
salt, to taste

preparation time 10 minutes
cooking time 35 minutes
serves 4

1. Heat the oil in a heavy-based saucepan and fry the cumin seeds over a medium heat until they start to darken.

2. Add the rice, mung dal, carrots, spices and water. Sprinkle in the turmeric and salt and bring to the boil, stirring all the time.

3. Reduce the heat to its lowest setting, cover with a lid and simmer gently for about 25 minutes, or until the rice is creamy and cooked. Remove the lid and pour in some more water, if necessary, to adjust the consistency – the rice should be very moist. Lift the spices out and serve with natural yogurt and hot lime or mango pickle.

MURGH DALCHINI PULAO

brown basmati with chicken, cinnamon and sunflower seeds

Brown rice retains the husk that surrounds the grain, making it chewier, nuttier and – unlike white rice – rich in nutrients such as B vitamins. It has more fibre than white rice, but takes longer to cook. I have combined it with cinnamon, which is used in traditional medicine to boost the digestion, and sunflower seeds for texture and a burst of vitamin E.

2 tablespoons sunflower oil
2 x 2.5cm cinnamon sticks
300g skinless chicken breasts,
    cut into 2.5cm cubes
½ teaspoon turmeric powder
½ teaspoon chilli powder
4 tablespoons frozen peas
300g brown basmati rice,
    washed and drained
salt, to taste
2 tablespoons lemon juice
750ml water
1 tablespoon sunflower seeds

preparation time 5 minutes
cooking time 35 minutes
serves 4

1. Heat the oil in a large, heavy-based saucepan and fry the cinnamon sticks for 30 seconds over a high heat to release their flavour. Add the chicken and stir-fry for 2–3 minutes to seal the meat.

2. Stir in the powdered spices and peas, and then add the rice. Stir gently and season with salt and lemon juice.

3. Pour in the water and bring to the boil. Reduce the heat, cover with a lid and cook for 25 minutes until the rice and chicken are done. Turn off the heat and leave the pan, covered, for a further 5 minutes.

4. Meanwhile, heat a small frying pan and dry-roast the sunflower seeds without any oil to make them crunchy – about 1 minute.

5. Uncover the rice and sprinkle with the sunflower seeds.

a healthy Sunday lunch

- brown basmati with chicken, cinnamon and sunflower seeds (MURGH DALCHINI PULAO)
- aubergine and chickpea curry (BAINGAN CHOLAY MASALA), page 87
- spinach and garlic raita (PALAK KA RAITA), page 140
- steamed rice and coconut parcels (MODAK), page 170

SAMUNDARI CHAVAL

spiced seafood and rice medley

This dish is the Indian version of paella. It is fragrant, spicy and very healthy with its combination of carbohydrate and protein. I sometimes make it simply with king prawns, adding cashew nuts for a bit of crunch.

3 tablespoons sunflower oil
1 teaspoon cumin seeds
1 large onion, finely chopped
1 teaspoon ginger-garlic paste
   (see page 173)
2 small green chillies, finely chopped
150g mixed seafood (e.g. prawns,
   squid, mussels, etc.)
300g basmati rice, washed
   and drained
1 teaspoon garam masala
2 ripe tomatoes, roughly chopped
salt, to taste
handful fresh coriander leaves,
   washed and finely chopped
600ml hot water

preparation time 15 minutes
cooking time 25 minutes
serves 4

1. Heat the oil in a large, heavy-based saucepan and fry the cumin seeds until they darken slightly. Add the onion and cook over a high heat for 5 minutes until soft. Add the ginger-garlic paste and chillies, and then carefully stir in the mixed seafood.

2. Add the rice with the garam masala and stir to coat it in the oil and spices. Add the tomatoes, salt and half the fresh coriander.

3. Pour in the hot water and bring to the boil, and then reduce the heat, cover with a lid and simmer gently for 10 minutes.

4. To serve, fluff up the rice with a fork and sprinkle with the remaining coriander.

MAKAI DHANIYE KI ROTI

corn and coriander bread

Corn bread is very popular in the northern state of Punjab. It is traditionally eaten with mustard greens cooked with onions, ginger and garlic. The dough can be quite sticky to handle, so it is best to roll out the rotis between sheets of greaseproof paper. Take extra care when lifting them onto the hot griddle.

225g coarse cornmeal
100g fine cornmeal
handful fresh coriander leaves,
   washed and finely chopped
salt, to taste
water, as required
wholewheat flour ('atta'),
   for dusting
greaseproof paper

preparation time 10 minutes
cooking time 30 minutes
makes 8 rotis

1. Combine the cornmeals with the fresh coriander and salt in a mixing bowl. Mix with enough water to form a stiff dough and knead until smooth. Divide into 8 evenly sized balls.

2. Place a sheet of greaseproof paper on your work surface and dust it with flour. Place a dough ball on top and cover with a second sheet of greaseproof paper. Roll out the dough between the sheets of greaseproof paper to form a disc 10cm in diameter.

3. Heat your griddle or large, shallow frying pan over a high heat and carefully lift the cornmeal roti on top. Be careful because it will tear very easily. Cook for 2–3 minutes, or until the surface bubbles up, and then turn over and cook on the other side. When cooked, the rotis should be flecked with brown spots all over.

4. Wrap in foil to keep warm while you roll out and cook the remaining rotis in the same way.

NAAN ⊙

baked yeast bread

Although naans are traditionally made in a clay oven called a tandoor, this version can be baked in the oven. The reason naan bread takes longer to make than parathas or rotis is that the dough contains yeast, which needs time to activate. Once the dough has risen, however, the naans are really easy to roll out and bake.

160ml warm water
1 teaspoon dried yeast
1 teaspoon sugar
380g self-raising flour
salt, to taste
2 tablespoons sunflower oil
30ml natural, low-fat yogurt

preparation time 20 minutes
  (+ 1½ hours raising time)
cooking time 20 minutes
makes 12 naan breads

1. Place the water, yeast and sugar in a small bowl and whisk together to dissolve the yeast. Leave to stand for 5 minutes.

2. Sift the flour and salt into a large mixing bowl. Pour in the yeast mixture, oil and yogurt, and mix to a soft dough with your hands. Turn onto a floured work surface and knead for 5 minutes until smooth.

3. Place the dough in a greased bowl, cover with clingfilm and leave to stand in a warm place for 1½ hours, or until the dough has doubled in size.

4. Preheat your oven to 200°C/400°F/gas mark 5, or turn your grill onto high. Punch the dough down with your fist, and then transfer it to a floured work surface and knead well for a couple of minutes. Divide into 12 balls and roll into flat discs, 15cm in diameter – you will need to keep flouring your surface to stop the naan from sticking.

5. Grease a baking tray and arrange the naans on top. Either bake in the oven for 10 minutes, or place under a hot grill for 2 minutes on each side, or until puffy and cooked.

DANEDAR ROTI

seed bread

At one of my bespoke cooking classes, I was asked to make rotis (traditional Indian flat breads) at very short notice. The only flour I had available was seeded bread flour and so I experimented with it. The rotis were delicious and now I often use seeded flour when making them. If you have difficulty finding it, simply add a tablespoon of crushed mixed seeds to ordinary wholemeal bread flour.

450g wholemeal, seeded bread flour
warm water, as required
1 teaspoon sunflower oil, plus extra
   for brushing

preparation time 10 minutes
cooking time 30 minutes
makes 10 rotis

1. Using your fingers, mix the flour with enough warm water to form a pliable dough. Turn onto a floured work surface and knead for 5 minutes – the more you knead the dough, the softer the rotis. Add 1 teaspoon oil and knead again.

2. Divide the dough into 10 portions, roughly the size of a lime. Coat lightly with flour, and then shape into balls in the palms of your hands and flatten slightly.

3. Roll out into flat discs, 10cm in diameter, flouring the surface as necessary.

4. Heat a griddle or large, shallow frying pan over a high heat. Roast the rotis one at a time on the hot griddle, waiting until the surface bubbles up before turning them over and cooking on the underside. To ensure they cook evenly, press down around the edges with the back of a flat spoon. As soon as brown spots appear on the underside, the rotis are done. Lightly brush with oil (optional) and wrap in foil to keep warm.

PALAK ROTI 🔥 🌀

spinach flavoured bread

Rotis are cooked in almost every home in India on a daily basis. In some parts of the country, they are called chapattis. Rotis vary in texture and size from one region of India to another. In the north, they are thicker, whereas in the western state of Gujarat, where the cuisine is quite delicate, they are smaller and thinner. Flavourings can be added to the basic roti dough to enhance the taste and nutritive value.

450g wholewheat flour ('atta'),
   available from Indian grocers
2 handfuls fresh spinach, washed,
   cooked and puréed
warm water, as required
1 teaspoon sunflower oil, plus extra
   for brushing

preparation time 10 minutes
cooking time 25 minutes
makes 12 rotis

1. Place the flour and spinach in a bowl and mix with enough water to form a pliable dough. Knead for 5 minutes, and then add the oil and knead again – the more you knead the dough, the softer the rotis.

2. Divide the dough into 12 equal portions and dust lightly with flour. Shape into balls in the palms of your hand and flatten slightly, and then roll out to form flat discs, 10cm in diameter.

3. Heat a griddle or large, shallow frying pan over a high heat. Cook the rotis on the griddle one at a time, turning them over when the surface bubbles up and brown specks appear on the underside. If necessary, press down around the edges with the back of a spoon to ensure they cook evenly.

4. Once they are cooked, brush with oil (optional) and then wrap in foil to keep warm while you cook the rest.

a quick family supper

- spinach flavoured bread (PALAK ROTI)
- beetroot with red kidney beans (CHUKANDAR KI SUBZI), page 91
- coriander and peanut chutney (DHANIYE KI CHUTNEY), page 149

KHEEME KE PARATHE

lamb mince stuffed bread

In northern India, bread is made with a variety of vegetarian fillings, including spiced potato, cauliflower, turnip and mooli. Lamb paratha is very popular in the southern state of Kerala, and it is much richer in flavour.

FOR THE FILLING:
1 tablespoon sunflower oil
½ teaspoon cumin seeds
1 teaspoon ginger-garlic paste
  (see page 173)
2 green chillies, finely chopped
150g lean minced lamb
½ teaspoon turmeric powder
½ teaspoon garam masala
salt, to taste
2 tablespoons finely chopped
  fresh coriander leaves

FOR THE BREAD:
450g wholewheat flour ('atta'),
  available from Indian grocers
2 tablespoons sunflower oil,
  plus extra for cooking
salt, to taste
water, as required

preparation time 20 minutes
cooking time 45 minutes
makes 8 parathas

1. To make the filling, heat 1 tablespoon oil in a heavy-based saucepan and fry the cumin seeds until slightly dark. Add the ginger-garlic paste, chillies, minced lamb, turmeric, garam masala and salt, and stir over a high heat for 2–3 minutes to seal the meat. Once the mince starts to bubble, turn down the heat, cover with a lid and simmer gently for 15 minutes. When the meat is cooked, take off the lid and boil rapidly so that any liquid evaporates. Stir in the fresh coriander and place on one side.

2. To make the dough, combine the flour with 2 tablespoons oil and a pinch of salt. Mix to a firm dough with water and knead until smooth.

3. Divide the dough into 16 evenly-sized balls. Roll each one out to form a flat disc, 8cm in diameter, dusting your surface with flour to prevent the mixture from sticking.

4. To assemble the parathas, place a heaped tablespoon of the filling in the centre of one of the circles of dough and smear out to the edges with the back of a spoon. Place another circle of dough on top and press down firmly around the edges to seal.

5. Heat a griddle or large, shallow frying pan over a high heat and dot with oil. Cook the paratha for 2–3 minutes on each side, or until tiny, dark spots appear on the underside, and then wrap in foil to keep warm while you cook the rest. Serve with any leftover mince on the side.

BAJRE KE PARATHE

pearl millet paratha with a potato and coriander filling

Pearl millet is a small grain that is ground into flour for making bread. The flour is very high in protein and much coarser than wholemeal flour, making for chunkier bread. Pearl millet and wholewheat flour ('atta') are both available from Indian grocers.

When forming the parathas, I find it easiest to pat them out on a sheet of plastic – a clean freezer bag will do – to prevent the dough from sticking to the work surface. The parathas are delicious served with natural yogurt.

150g pearl millet flour
150g wholewheat flour ('atta')
200ml water
handful fresh coriander leaves, washed and finely chopped
2 medium potatoes, boiled with the skins on, then peeled and mashed
salt, to taste
juice of 1 lemon
½ teaspoon ground cumin
sunflower oil, for brushing

preparation time 10 minutes
cooking time 40 minutes
makes 8 parathas

1. Combine the flours in a large mixing bowl and make a well in the centre. Pour in the water and mix to a soft dough. Knead for about 5 minutes.

2. To make the filling, combine the fresh coriander, mashed potato, salt, lemon juice and cumin in a separate bowl and mix well together. Divide this mixture into 8 portions.

3. Shape the dough into eight evenly-sized balls. Line your work surface with a clean sheet of plastic and place a dough ball on top. Wet your palms and pat the dough into a disc, 10cm in diameter. Place a portion of the potato filling in the centre and gather up the edges of the paratha around it to enclose the filling. Seal the dough on top.

4. Carefully transfer the stuffed ball of dough onto a floured work surface and gently roll it out to a disc, 15cm in diameter.

5. Heat your griddle or large, shallow frying pan over a high heat. Gently lift the paratha onto the griddle and cook for 3–4 minutes on each side. To ensure it cooks evenly, press it down with the back of a spoon – especially around the edges.

6. Once it is done, brush the paratha lightly with sunflower oil and wrap it in foil to keep warm while you cook the rest.

BESAN KI ROTI ⬤ ⬤

gram flour pancakes

Gram flour is made from chickpeas. It is mainly used as a thickener in some curries or to make batter for coating vegetables or fish. It is rich in carbohydrates, but has no gluten – making it perfect for those with a gluten allergy. I love this bread because it is simple to make, is quite filling and can be eaten on its own.

1 small onion, finely chopped
1 ripe tomato, finely chopped
2 tablespoons finely chopped
   fresh coriander leaves
½ green pepper, finely diced
50g cabbage, coarsely grated
¼ teaspoon ground cumin
200g gram flour (available from
   Indian grocers or the Asian section
   of some supermarkets)
salt, to taste
water, as required
a little sunflower oil, for cooking

preparation time 15 minutes
cooking time 15 minutes
makes 8 pancakes

1. Combine the onion, tomato, fresh coriander, green pepper, cabbage, cumin, gram flour and salt in a bowl and mix well together. Add the water a little at a time, stirring between each addition, to give a batter the same consistency as thick custard.

2. Heat a griddle or large, shallow frying pan over a high heat and dot with oil. Ladle a spoonful of the batter onto the hot surface and flatten with the back of a spoon to form a 10cm pancake. Cook for 2–3 minutes, or until golden, and then flip over and cook on the underside with some more oil. Wrap in foil to keep warm while you cook the rest of the pancakes.

THALIPEETH

spiced multi-grain bread

This very nutritious bread is traditionally made in the state of Maharashtra using 'bhajani' flour, which is a combination of flours including pearl millet. The rotis are usually eaten with yogurt, but can be combined with any curry or dry vegetable dish.

The dough is quite sticky to handle, so it is best to roll out the rotis between sheets of greaseproof paper.

300g mixed flours to include gram flour ('besan'), rice flour, wholewheat flour ('atta') and semolina in
   equal quantities
½ teaspoon ground cumin
1 medium onion, finely chopped
2 green chillies, very finely chopped
handful fresh coriander leaves, washed and finely chopped
water, as required
greaseproof paper
sunflower oil, for brushing

preparation time 10 minutes
cooking time 25 minutes
makes 8 rotis

1. Combine the flours, cumin, onion, chillies and fresh coriander in a mixing bowl. Mix with enough water to form a stiff dough and knead until smooth. Divide into 8 evenly sized balls and dust with flour.

2. Place a sheet of greaseproof paper on your work surface and dust with flour. Place a dough ball on top and cover with a second sheet of greaseproof paper. Roll out the dough between the sheets of paper to form a disc, 10cm in diameter.

3. Heat a griddle or large, shallow frying pan and gently lift the roti on top. Pierce the roti all over with a fork so that it cooks evenly, and then dot the surface with oil. Cook for 2–3 minutes on each side, or until the bread is flecked with brown spots all over.

4. Wrap in foil to keep warm while you roll out and cook the rest.

two the curries

Few Indian meals are complete without a curry. I believe that the healthiest kind of curry is one made at home. I don't believe in using ready pastes because I'm never entirely sure of all the contents. Most curries are easy and quick to make. Here are a few points to consider when making a curry at home.

One of the most important things to get right is the consistency. A good curry should be fairly thick so that it moistens the accompanying bread or rice sufficiently. To prevent it from becoming too watery, make sure you don't add too much water at the beginning – you can always add more later on – and always lower the heat after the sauce has come to the boil to prevent it from drying out.

Think about the colour also. Turmeric, red chillies, tomatoes and garam masala are some of the ingredients that can be introduced to add colour. They add flavour and aroma as well, and many of them provide all-important healing and medicinal properties. All spices aid the digestion.

There are many different methods of making a curry, according to the region. A northern Indian curry would start with the heating of the oil. Then the seed spices are added to release their aromatic oils. The onions, ginger, garlic and tomatoes go in next to add moisture. The pan is now ready to receive the powdered spices so that they do not burn. The main ingredient follows, then salt and a little water to get the consistency right.

Thus curries are made in steps, almost like building blocks. The blocks can be moved around and rearranged in countless ways to give endless recipes.

meat curries

India is home to nearly all the world's religions. However, the vast majority of people living in India are Hindus and for religious reasons – the cow being considered sacred – do not eat beef. Not all Hindus are vegetarian, since caste and community also affect this choice. For example, some of my strict Brahmin ancestors ate fish simply because they lived near the coast around Goa.

Most non-vegetarians in India will eat meat or fish only once or twice a week – on the one hand, because it is expensive, and secondly, because there is so much choice of vegetables, lentils, beans and dairy produce. In deference to the Muslim population, pork is not popular either.

In India, the most popular non-vegetarian meals consist of chicken or 'mutton', which is usually in the form of goat (except in mountainous regions where lamb is also eaten). All the recipes in this chapter are made with lamb.

Ayurvedic wisdom

Lamb is considered to be unsettling for all the doshas and in order for it to be digested properly, it is essential to combine it with fruits, spices, vegetables and legumes that kindle the digestive fire or 'agni' and create energy in the body.

DHANSAK

lamb with lentils and vegetables

This typical Parsee dish is traditionally eaten with caramel and onion-flavoured brown rice. 'Dhan' means rice, while 'sak' is the combination of lamb and lentils. Although there are many ingredients in a dhansak, most of them are widely available – bottle gourds can be bought from most Indian grocers, but if you have trouble finding them you could substitute courgette instead. The dish couldn't be easier to prepare – the ingredients are simply combined in a saucepan and simmered for 40 minutes.

2 large onions, finely chopped
150g ripe tomatoes, roughly chopped
150g bottle gourd ('doodhai') or
    courgette, finely chopped
4 tablespoons red pumpkin,
    finely chopped
small handful fresh fenugreek
    leaves, finely chopped
handful fresh coriander leaves,
    finely chopped
handful mint leaves, finely chopped
150g split yellow lentils ('toor dal')
300g lean, boneless lamb, trimmed
    and cut into 2.5cm cubes
1 teaspoon turmeric powder
1 teaspoon chilli powder
salt, to taste
4 tablespoons distilled vinegar
1 tablespoon sunflower oil
1 teaspoon cumin seeds

preparation time 30 minutes
cooking time 1 hour
serves 4

1. Place all the ingredients except for the vinegar, sunflower oil and cumin seeds in a large, heavy-based saucepan. Cover with 450ml water and bring to the boil, stirring all the time. Reduce the heat and simmer for 40 minutes until the lamb is cooked and the lentils are soft.

2. Lightly mash the vegetables and lentils with a wooden spoon, taking care not to break up the meat. Stir in the vinegar.

3. Heat the oil in a small frying pan and fry the cumin seeds over a medium heat until lightly toasted. Pour over the curry.

BADAMI BAINGAN GOSHT 🐘 🔥

lamb and aubergine curry with almonds

This warming curry is an excellent choice when you need a bit of an energy boost. In Ayurveda, almonds are considered warming and restorative. I have combined them in this recipe with aubergines, which have a bitter taste ('rasa'). Aubergines are generally not salted or drained in Ayurvedic cooking because their bitter juices are needed to balance the other taste elements in the dish (see page 12).

Almond skins can be difficult to digest and this is why I remove them in many of my recipes. To remove the skins, simply soak the almonds in a little hot water for about half an hour and then slip them off with your fingers.

2 medium onions, roughly chopped
2.5cm piece fresh root ginger, scraped
4 garlic cloves, peeled
2 tablespoons sunflower oil
600g lean, boneless lamb, trimmed and cut into 2.5cm cubes
4 tablespoons whole almonds (skins removed), coarsely pounded with a pestle and mortar
1 large aubergine, cut into 2.5cm cubes
1 tablespoon garam masala
1 teaspoon turmeric powder
1 teaspoon chilli powder
salt, to taste
300ml natural, low-fat yogurt

preparation time 15 minutes
cooking time 45 minutes
serves 4

1. Place the onion, ginger and garlic in a blender and blitz to a smooth purée with 2–3 tablespoons water.

2. Heat the oil in a kadhai (or large, heavy-based saucepan) over a high heat and brown the lamb on all sides.

3. Add the mixture from the blender and stir over a low heat for 10 minutes to cook the onion. Add the almonds and aubergine.

4. Sprinkle in the spices and salt, and then pour in 150ml water. Bring to the boil, stirring all the time, and then simmer gently for 30 minutes until the lamb is cooked and the aubergine has collapsed.

5. Take off the heat and stir in the yogurt.

minced lamb with mushrooms and peas

I like to use chestnut mushrooms in this recipe because they are chunkier and chewier than closed cup mushrooms. Any leftover curry can be rolled up in a wrap or eaten with pasta or a baked potato.

1 tablespoon sunflower oil

1 medium onion, finely chopped

2 teaspoons ginger-garlic paste (see page 173)

2 tablespoons tomato purée

300g lean minced lamb

150g garden peas (shelled weight), fresh or frozen

150g chestnut mushrooms, cleaned and roughly chopped

½ teaspoon chilli powder

½ teaspoon turmeric powder

½ teaspoon ground coriander

1 teaspoon garam masala

salt, to taste

2 tablespoons finely chopped fresh coriander leaves

preparation time 5 minutes
cooking time 25 minutes
serves 4

1. Heat the oil in a kadhai or heavy-based saucepan and fry the onion over a high heat until soft and just beginning to turn golden.

2. Stir in the ginger-garlic paste and tomato purée and cook for 1 minute.

3. Add the minced lamb, peas, mushrooms, powdered spices and salt and stir well to seal the meat. When the mince begins to bubble, turn down the heat, cover with a lid and simmer gently for about 15 minutes, or until the lamb is cooked.

4. Serve hot, garnished with fresh coriander.

METHI GOSHT

lamb with fenugreek

I love fenugreek for its slightly bittersweet taste and strong curry flavour. Also it is very high in calcium. Fresh fenugreek is available tied in bunches from most Indian grocers. To prepare it, simply break off the leaves along with their tender stalks and discard the thick stem.

2 tablespoons sunflower oil
2 medium onions, roughly chopped
2 teaspoons ginger-garlic paste
  (see page 173)
1 ripe tomato, roughly chopped
1 tablespoon tomato purée
2 green chillies, very finely chopped
600g lean, boneless lamb, trimmed
  and cut into 2.5cm cubes
2 handfuls fresh fenugreek leaves,
  washed and finely chopped (or 2
  tablespoons dried fenugreek
  leaves)
salt, to taste
1 teaspoon turmeric powder
1 teaspoon ground coriander
1 teaspoon ground cumin
1 teaspoon garam masala

preparation time 15 minutes
cooking time 40 minutes
serves 4

1. Heat 1 tablespoon oil in a frying pan and add the onions. Fry over a high heat for 5 minutes until slightly brown, and then add the ginger-garlic paste, chopped tomato, tomato purée and green chillies. Fry together for a couple of minutes until mushy, and then transfer the mixture to a blender and blitz to a fine purée with 2–3 tablespoons water.

2. Meanwhile, heat 1 tablespoon oil in a heavy-based saucepan and fry the lamb over a high heat for 2–3 minutes to seal the meat. Add the fenugreek, salt and powdered spices and mix well.

3. Pour in the mixture from the blender and top up with enough water to barely cover the lamb. Bring to the boil, stirring all the time. Cover with a lid and simmer gently over a low heat for 30 minutes until the lamb is cooked.

DAL GOSHT

lean lamb with spiced lentils

This dish comes from Hyderabad and is traditionally made with ghee and lots of spices. I have simplified the recipe to make it easier and healthier. The creaminess of the lentils complements the lamb beautifully and also provides valuable protein, carbohydrate and fibre.

150g split yellow gram lentils ('chana dal')
2 tablespoons sunflower oil
2 large onions, finely chopped
2 teaspoons ginger-garlic paste (see page 173)
2 green chillies, finely chopped
3 ripe tomatoes, roughly chopped
600g lean, boneless lamb, trimmed and cut into 2.5cm cubes
1 teaspoon turmeric powder
1 teaspoon ground coriander
1 teaspoon garam masala
salt, to taste
3 teaspoons lemon juice
small handful fresh coriander leaves, washed and finely chopped

preparation time 10 minutes
cooking time 50 minutes
serves 4

1. Place the lentils in a saucepan and cover with double their volume of water. Bring to the boil, and then reduce the heat and simmer for 30 minutes until mushy.

2. Meanwhile, heat 1 tablespoon oil in a heavy-based frying pan and fry the onions over a high heat until slightly brown. Add the ginger-garlic paste, green chillies and tomatoes. Cook for 3–4 minutes until the tomatoes are mushy, and then transfer the mixture to a blender and blitz to a fine paste with about 4 tablespoons water.

3. Heat 1 tablespoon oil in a heavy-based saucepan and seal the meat over a high heat. Add the powdered spices and season with salt.

4. Pour in the mixture from the blender and top up with 300ml water. Bring to the boil, and then reduce the heat and simmer gently for 30 minutes until the lamb is tender. You may need to add a little more water if the curry starts to dry out.

5. Add the cooked lentils and combine thoroughly, and then stir in the lemon juice and fresh coriander.

MASALE KE KOFTE

meatballs in a fennel and ginger curry

Fennel is classed as cooling and sweet by Ayurveda, and it is often chewed after an Indian meal to help digestion. In India, ginger is called 'maha aushadhi', or great medicine, because it is said to cure so many ailments.

2 teaspoons fennel seeds
600g lean minced lamb
3 garlic cloves, peeled and finely grated
salt, to taste
2 tablespoons sunflower oil
2 medium onions, finely chopped
2.5cm piece fresh root ginger, skin scraped
1 fresh green chilli
1 teaspoon turmeric powder
1 teaspoon garam masala
3 tablespoons natural, low-fat yogurt

preparation time 10 minutes
cooking time 30 minutes
serves 4

1. Place the fennel seeds in a small frying pan and dry-roast them over a low heat until they start to darken. Tip them into a mortar and grind to a powder.

2. Combine the minced lamb, garlic, salt and half the roasted fennel powder in a mixing bowl and form into cherry-sized meatballs.

3. To make the curry sauce, heat the oil in a heavy-based saucepan and fry the onions over a high heat until soft. Finely chop the ginger and chillies and add to the pan. Continue cooking for 1 minute, and then transfer the mixture to a blender and blitz to a fine purée with 4–5 tablespoons water. Add the turmeric, garam masala and the rest of the dry-roasted fennel powder.

4. Meanwhile, heat a non-stick frying pan with a lid over a medium heat and arrange the meatballs inside. Add the mixture from the blender, thinning it if necessary with enough water to make it pouring consistency. Season with salt.

5. Bring to the boil, turning the meatballs carefully to make sure they are sealed on all sides. Reduce the heat, cover with a lid and simmer for about 15 minutes, or until the meatballs are cooked through. Take off the heat and stir in the yogurt.

lamb curry with coconut and curry leaves

Curry leaves are greatly valued in Ayurveda because of their high vitamin and mineral content – they are rich in carotene, vitamin C, zinc and magnesium, to name but a few. Curry leaves are best eaten fresh, although they are more widely available in their dried form.

2 tablespoons sunflower oil
1 teaspoon coriander seeds
2 medium onions, roughly chopped
small handful fresh or dried
 curry leaves
2 teaspoons ginger-garlic paste
 (see page 173)
6 dried red chillies (seeds removed),
 soaked in warm water to soften
 the skins
600g lean, boneless lamb, trimmed
 and cut into 2.5cm cubes
1 teaspoon turmeric powder
1 teaspoon garam masala
salt, to taste
juice of 1 lemon
50ml coconut milk

preparation time 10 minutes
cooking time 50 minutes
serves 4

1. Heat 1 tablespoon oil in a frying pan and fry the coriander seeds until they start to darken. Add the onions and cook over a high heat for 5 minutes until soft.

2. Add the curry leaves and ginger-garlic paste, stirring well. Drain and add the whole red chillies, and fry for a couple of minutes until mushy. Transfer the mixture to a blender and blitz to a fine purée with a few tablespoons water.

3. Meanwhile, heat the remaining tablespoon oil in a heavy-based saucepan and add the lamb. Fry over a high heat to seal the meat, and then add the powdered spices and salt.

4. Add the mixture from the blender, along with enough water to barely cover the lamb. Bring to the boil, stirring all the time, and then cover and cook on a low heat for about 30 minutes, or until the lamb is cooked. Stir in the lemon juice.

5. To finish, pour in the coconut milk and heat through.

GOSHT KA KORMA 🌸

lamb in a cashew nut curry

Cashew nuts are high in fibre and protein, as well as in monounsaturated or 'good' fats, and they have no cholesterol. They are rich in calories, however – about 100g of cashew nuts can contain as many as 600 calories!

FOR THE MARINADE:
2 medium onions, roughly chopped
3 teaspoons ginger-garlic paste
   (see page 173)
2 green chillies, finely chopped
150ml natural, low-fat yoghurt
salt, to taste
600g lean, boneless lamb, trimmed
   and cut into 2.5cm cubes
3 tablespoons sunflower oil
1 teaspoon ground coriander
1 teaspoon ground cumin
1 teaspoon garam masala
100g unsalted cashew nuts, ground
   to a paste with a little water in
   a blender
50ml coconut milk

preparation time 10 minutes
   (+ 15 minutes marinating time)
cooking time 50 minutes
serves 4

1. To make the marinade, place the onions, ginger-garlic paste and chilli in a blender and blitz to a fine puree with 3–4 tablespoons water. Transfer to a large mixing bowl and stir in the yoghurt and salt. Add the lamb, coating it well in the mixture, and marinate for 15 minutes.

2. Heat the oil in a large, heavy-based saucepan. Lift the lamb out of the marinade and add it to the pan. Stir well over a high heat to sear the meat, and then add the powdered spices.

3. Pour in the marinade and top up with 120ml water. Bring to the boil, stirring all the time. Reduce the heat, cover with a lid and simmer gently for about 30 minutes, or until the lamb is cooked.

4. To finish, stir in the cashew nut paste and coconut milk and heat through.

chicken curries

Chicken is rich in essential amino acids that cannot be synthesized in the body. It can be an extremely low-fat food if it is eaten without its skin. Chicken is high in niacin, one of the important B vitamins, as well as minerals such as selenium and phosphorous.

ayurvedic wisdom

White meat such as chicken is acceptable to Vata and Pitta, but can aggravate Kapha. Chicken has light, sweet and astringent qualities and it is classed as a heating meat.

MURGH MASALA PANKHARI

chicken wings in a pepper and cumin sauce

Pepper, which changed the history of the world, was used to spice up curries long before the Portuguese introduced chillies to India. A pungent spice that promotes good appetite and can reduce flatulence, pepper has always been greatly valued in India for its digestive properties. Here, I have combined it with cumin to make a really simple, quick dish that can be served as a main course with rice, or as a starter with a side salad.

2 tablespoons sunflower oil
1 tablespoon ginger-garlic paste
 (see page 173)
1 teaspoon coarsely ground
 black pepper
1 tablespoon ground cumin
600g skinless chicken wings
salt, to taste
3 tablespoons finely chopped
 fresh coriander leaves
50ml coconut milk

preparation time 10 minutes
cooking time 25 minutes
serves 4

1. Heat the oil in a kadhai (or heavy-based saucepan) and add the ginger-garlic paste. Stir over a high heat for about a minute.

2. Add the pepper and cumin and then the chicken wings.

3. Season with salt and stir to coat the chicken with the spices. Add about 4 tablespoons water and bring to the boil. Reduce the heat, cover with a lid and simmer gently for 10–15 minutes, or until the chicken is cooked through.

4. Remove the lid, increase the heat and continue cooking until most of the liquid has dried up. Stir in the fresh coriander.

an Indian picnic

- chicken wings in a pepper and cumin sauce (MURGH MASALA PANKHARI)
- quinoa stir-fried with spices and vegetables (QUINOA UPMA), page 120
- spiced chickpea salad (CHANNA CHAAT), page 145
- orange and semolina pudding with saffron (SANTRE KA SHEERA), page 165

MURGH SUBZ BAHAR

herby chicken and vegetable curry

I have made countless versions of this healthy recipe and I am constantly experimenting with different vegetables for variety. As an alternative to peppers and spinach, try using broccoli or spring greens. I always use skinless chicken drumsticks.

FOR THE CURRY PASTE:
1 bunch fresh mint, washed
1 bunch fresh coriander, washed and roughly chopped
2 green chillies, finely chopped
2 teaspoons ginger-garlic paste (see page 173)
1 green pepper (stalk and seeds removed), roughly chopped
2 big handfuls spinach, washed and roughly chopped

2 tablespoons sunflower oil
600g skinless chicken drumsticks
1 teaspoon garam masala
1 teaspoon turmeric powder
salt, to taste

preparation time 15 minutes
cooking time 35 minutes
serves 4

1. Remove a few of the mint leaves to use as a garnish. Roughly chop the rest of the mint and place it in the blender with the remaining ingredients for the curry paste. Whizz to a smooth paste with about 100ml water.

2. Heat the oil in a heavy-based saucepan and fry the chicken over a high heat until sealed. Add the garam masala and turmeric. Season with salt.

3. Pour in the green curry paste and top up with enough water to almost cover the chicken. Bring to the boil, and then reduce the heat and cover with a lid. Simmer very gently for about 20 minutes, or until the chicken is cooked through.

4. Remove the lid, increase the heat and boil rapidly to thicken the curry sauce so that it coats the chicken. Garnish with fresh mint leaves.

DAKSHINI MURGH

south-Indian-style chicken with peas

South-Indian cooking uses coconut, which grows in abundance in the region, as well as spices such as peppercorns and fennel. The fennel seeds add sweetness to the dish, balancing the hot and bitter flavours of the other ingredients, such as the green chillies and cumin. Fennel is classed as a cooling spice in Ayurveda and it is widely used in digestive tonics.

2 tablespoons sunflower oil
½ teaspoon cumin seeds
½ teaspoon fennel seeds
10 black peppercorns, crushed
1 large onion, finely sliced
2 teaspoons ginger-garlic paste (see page 173)
2 green chillies, very finely chopped
½ teaspoon turmeric powder
600g skinless chicken breasts, cut into 2.5cm cubes
4 tablespoons frozen peas
2 ripe tomatoes, finely chopped
salt, to taste
3 tablespoons desiccated coconut

preparation time 10 minutes
cooking time 30 minutes
serves 4

1. Heat the oil in a heavy-based saucepan over a medium heat. Add the cumin, fennel seeds and black pepper and fry together for 1 minute to release their flavours. Add the onion and fry until soft – about 5 minutes.

2. Add the ginger-garlic paste and green chillies and stir for a few seconds.

3. Add the turmeric powder, chicken and peas and stir-fry for about 5 minutes to seal the meat. Add the tomatoes and season with salt.

4. Give everything a good stir, and then pour in 3–4 tablespoons hot water to prevent the chicken from sticking. Cover with a lid, reduce the heat and simmer gently for 12–15 minutes, or until the chicken is cooked through. Stir in the coconut and serve hot.

KASTURI MURGH

chicken curry with almonds and fenugreek

Dried fenugreek leaves ('kasuri methi') are slightly bitter in taste and are therefore helpful in getting rid of 'ama' or toxic substances from the body. Ayurveda believes that bitter tastes reduce the 'med-dhatu' or fatty tissues and help with weight loss. Also, fenugreek is also excellent for the digestion and improves the function of the liver.

12 skinless chicken drumsticks
150ml natural, low-fat yogurt
salt, to taste
60g whole almonds, soaked in hot water for 10 minutes to soften the skins
2 tablespoons sunflower oil
1 teaspoon cumin seeds
1 teaspoon dried fenugreek ('kasuri methi')
2 medium onions, finely chopped
2 teaspoons ginger-garlic paste (see page 173)
2 tablespoons tomato purée
½ teaspoon chilli powder
1 teaspoon turmeric powder
1 tablespoon garam masala

preparation time 15 minutes
cooking time 35 minutes
serves 4

1. Marinate the chicken in the yogurt and salt while you prepare the rest of the ingredients.

2. Skin the almonds and blitz them with some water in a blender to make a coarse purée.

3. Heat a heavy-based saucepan and add the oil. Sprinkle in the cumin seeds and fry over a medium heat for a few seconds until they start to darken.

4. Add the fenugreek and then the onions and stir-fry over a high heat until soft – about 5 minutes. Add the ginger-garlic paste.

5. Lift the chicken out of the marinade and add it to the pan. Stir well to seal the meat on all sides – about 2–3 minutes.

6. Add the tomato purée, the rest of the yogurt marinade and the powdered spices. Scoop in the puréed almonds and top up with 100ml water. Season with salt. Bring to the boil, stirring all the time, and then reduce the heat and cover with a lid. Simmer for about 30 minutes until the chicken is cooked through, stirring from time to time to ensure the nut purée does not stick to the bottom of the pan.

---

a calming menu for Vata (see page 9)

- chicken curry with almonds and fenugreek (KASTURI MURGH)
- seed bread (DANEDAR ROTI), page 27
- aubergine mash with peanuts (BAINGAN MOONGPHALI BHARTA), page 106

KOZHI KARI

Kerala-style chicken and cardamom curry

Cardamom is an important spice used in both savoury and sweet recipes. Ayurveda considers its fragrance to be uplifting and uses it as an antidepressant. Cardamom-flavoured tea is said to relieve tension headaches, while chewing on its seeds is a cure for bad breath, travel sickness and dizziness.

2 tablespoons sunflower oil
6 fresh curry leaves, plus extra
   for garnishing
2 medium onions, finely chopped
2 teaspoons ginger-garlic paste
   (see page 173)
2 green chillies, finely chopped
2 ripe tomatoes, roughly chopped
1 teaspoon turmeric powder
½ teaspoon ground cardamom –
   simply remove the husks from 6
   whole green cardamom pods and
   crush the seeds to a powder
600g skinless chicken breasts,
   cut into 2.5cm cubes
1 tablespoon tamarind paste,
   mixed with 2–3 tablespoons water
salt, to taste
50ml coconut milk

preparation time 10 minutes
cooking time 35 minutes
serves 4

1. Heat the oil in a heavy-based saucepan over a medium heat. Add 6 curry leaves and fry them for 10 seconds until they start to colour and release their fragrance.

2. Add the onions and stir-fry until soft – about 5 minutes. Stir in the ginger-garlic paste.

3. Add the chillies and the tomatoes and stir-fry for 2–3 minutes, or until mushy and well blended. Sprinkle in the turmeric and ground cardamom.

4. Drop in the pieces of chicken and fry over a high heat to seal the meat on all sides. Pour in the tamarind, season with salt and bring to the boil.

5. Reduce the heat, cover with a lid and simmer gently for about 15 minutes, or until the chicken is cooked. Pour in the coconut milk and heat through. Serve hot, garnished with a few curry leaves.

chicken and potato curry with egg drops

Bay leaves are one of the ingredients in garam masala (literally translated as 'hot spice'), the special blend of warming spices that is widely used in northern Indian cooking (see page 173). According to Ayurveda, bay leaves have an astringent 'rasa' or taste and are excellent for the digestion. They are also high in iron and vitamin A. Bay leaves are readily available in their dried form and will keep well for 6–8 months.

2 tablespoons sunflower oil
2 medium onions, finely sliced
2 teaspoons ginger-garlic paste
 (see page 173)
3 ripe tomatoes, roughly chopped
2 bay leaves
600g skinless chicken breasts,
 cut into 2.5cm cubes
1 potato, peeled and coarsely grated
½ teaspoon chilli powder
1 teaspoon turmeric powder
1 teaspoon garam masala
salt, to taste
2 large eggs, beaten
2 tablespoons finely chopped
 fresh coriander leaves

preparation time 15 minutes
cooking time 30 minutes
serves 4

1. Heat 1 tablespoon oil in a heavy-based saucepan, add the onions and fry over a high heat until soft. Add the ginger-garlic paste and tomatoes. Cook for a few minutes until the tomatoes are mushy.

2. Transfer the mixture to a blender and blitz to a coarse paste with 3–4 tablespoons water.

3. Rinse out the pan and heat the remaining tablespoon of oil. Add the bay leaves and then the chicken and stir-fry over a medium heat to seal the meat on all sides.

4. Add the grated potato and spice powders and give everything a good stir. Scoop in the mixture from the blender and season with salt. Add 100ml water and bring to the boil, stirring all the time to prevent the potato from sticking to the pan.

5. Reduce the heat, cover with a lid and simmer for 15 minutes until the chicken is cooked through.

6. Take off the lid and move the chicken to one side of the pan. Beat the eggs into the curry sauce with a fork so that they cook in tiny shreds. Garnish with fresh coriander.

MURGH SOWETA

chicken with sweetcorn

This recipe is bursting with the flavour of tomatoes, both fresh and concentrated. Tomatoes are said to lower the risk of many different kinds of cancer. This may be due to lycopene, the chemical that makes tomatoes red. It is thought that eating tomatoes with a small amount of fat enables lycopene to be absorbed better. Tomatoes are very rich in the antioxidant vitamin C and they can help reduce the risk of heart disease.

2 tablespoons sunflower oil
2 medium onions, finely chopped
2 teaspoons ginger-garlic paste
   (see page 173)
600g skinless chicken breasts, cut
   into 2.5cm cubes
150g sweetcorn, fresh or frozen
½ teaspoon chilli powder
1 teaspoon garam masala
½ teaspoon turmeric powder
225g ripe tomatoes, roughly chopped
1 tablespoon tomato purée
salt, to taste
2 tablespoons finely chopped fresh
   coriander leaves, to garnish

preparation time 10 minutes
cooking time 30 minutes
serves 4

1. Heat the oil in a heavy-based, non-stick saucepan and fry the onions over a high heat until soft – about 5 minutes. Add the ginger-garlic paste and fry for 1 minute.

2. Add the chicken and stir-fry for 5 minutes to seal the meat.

3. Add the rest of the ingredients and continue cooking until the chicken is cooked through – about 15 minutes. You may need to add a little water, to prevent the curry from drying up.

4. Garnish with fresh coriander.

VINDALOO 🌀 🔥

Goan-style chicken curry

The Portuguese first brought vindaloo – a sweet, sour and hot curry – to India, although their version contained red wine, as well as chillies and garlic. Contrary to popular belief outside India, the term vindaloo is not a measure of heat. The dish is not popular all over India; it is eaten mainly in Goa, which was a stronghold of the Portuguese.

¼ teaspoon mustard seeds
5 black peppercorns
1 teaspoon coriander seeds
1 teaspoon cumin seeds
2 dried red chillies (seeds removed)
2 tablespoons sunflower oil
2 medium onions, finely chopped
2 teaspoons ginger-garlic paste
   (see page 173)
1 small green chilli, finely chopped
1 teaspoon garam masala
600g skinless chicken breasts,
   cut into 2.5cm cubes
1 tablespoon tamarind paste,
   mixed with 2–3 tablespoons water
3 teaspoons malt vinegar
½ teaspoon brown sugar
salt, to taste

preparation time 10 minutes
cooking time 35 minutes
serves 4

1. Combine the mustard seeds, peppercorns, coriander seeds, cumin seeds and dried red chillies in a bowl. Heat a small frying pan and dry-roast this spice mixture for a couple of minutes over a medium heat until the seeds start to darken and release their fragrance. Transfer them to a small blender or coffee mill and blitz to a powder.

2. Heat the oil in a heavy-based saucepan and fry the onions over a high heat until they are well browned. Add the ginger-garlic paste and fry together for 1 minute.

3. Add the green chilli, dry-roasted spice powder and garam masala. Drop in the pieces of chicken and stir-fry for 5 minutes to seal the meat on all sides.

4. Pour in the tamarind and vinegar, add the sugar and season with salt. Add about 100ml water and bring to the boil. Reduce the heat, cover with a lid and simmer gently for about 20 minutes, or until the chicken is cooked through and the sauce is thick and fragrant.

KADHAI MURGH

chicken with coriander

A 'kadhai' is a heavy, wok-shaped utensil which is found in most Indian kitchens. It is usually made of a metal alloy, which enables it to withstand the high temperatures required for Indian cooking. A well-seasoned kadhai – that is, one that has been well used – will not let the food stick, even during long cooking times. 'Balti' cooking seems to have been inspired by the kadhai. Balti means 'bucket', but every balti dish I have ever eaten has been served in a kadhai!

1 teaspoon coriander seeds
1 teaspoon cumin seeds
2 tablespoons sunflower oil
600g skinless chicken breasts,
    cut into 2.5cm cubes
2 teaspoons freshly grated root ginger
1 teaspoon freshly grated garlic
2 tablespoons tomato purée
2 ripe tomatoes, roughly chopped
2 green chillies, very finely chopped
2 big handfuls fresh coriander,
    washed and finely chopped
1 teaspoon turmeric powder
1 teaspoon garam masala
salt, to taste

preparation time 15 minutes
cooking time 30 minutes
serves 4

1. Heat a small frying pan and add the coriander and cumin seeds. Dry-roast them with no oil until they start to darken, and then transfer them to a mortar and crush to a powder.

2. Heat the oil in a kadhai (or heavy-based saucepan) and stir-fry the chicken over a high heat for about 5 minutes to seal the meat on all sides. Add the ginger and garlic and stir-fry for 1 minute. Add the tomato purée, chopped tomatoes and chillies and cook for 2–3 minutes, or until the tomatoes are mushy and the sauce is well blended.

3. Add the fresh coriander and the roasted coriander and cumin seed powder. Cook for a few minutes to blend, and then sprinkle in the turmeric and garam masala. Season with salt.

4. Add 3–4 tablespoons water and bring to the boil. Reduce the heat and simmer gently for about 15 minutes, or until the chicken is cooked through.

fish and seafood curries

Fish is low in fat and high in protein and contains vital omega-3 fatty acids. Studies show that we should all be eating at least two portions of fish a week. Oily fish, such as salmon and mackerel, are particularly beneficial and can help reduce the risk of cardiovascular disease. Eating fish regularly is also said to help with other health problems, such as asthma and dementia.

Although fish is a great source of minerals, the phosphorous present in most fish can upset reserves of bone-building calcium in our bodies. However, eating it with calcium-rich leafy greens is more balancing.

Ayurvedic wisdom

Fish is quite heating according to Ayurveda and therefore it is tolerated well by people with a Vata constitution. Pitta can enjoy white fish in moderation, but Kapha need to be careful with most sea fish – although they can tolerate prawns and river fish.

SABZIONWALI MACCHI

salmon with a spicy vegetable curry

Salmon is a wonderfully versatile fish with its creamy flavour and firm texture. Indian salmon or 'raavas' is slightly different from its Western counterpart, with white flesh and a distinctive taste of the sea. Both varieties are packed with protein and rich in omega-3 fats that protect the heart. They also contain selenium and vitamins B6 and B12. Wild salmon, if you can get hold of it, is rich in vitamin D too.

4 x 150g salmon fillets
2 tablespoons sunflower oil,
   plus extra for brushing
1 teaspoon cumin seeds
1 medium onion, finely chopped
2 red peppers (stalks and seeds
   removed), finely chopped
1 aubergine, cut into 2.5cm cubes
½ teaspoon chilli powder
½ teaspoon turmeric powder
1 teaspoon garam masala
2 large ripe tomatoes,
   roughly chopped
salt, to taste
1 tablespoon tomato purée
handful fresh coriander leaves,
   washed and finely chopped

preparation time 10 minutes
cooking time 20 minutes
serves 4

1. Preheat your oven to 220°C/425°F/gas mark 7.

2. Brush the salmon fillets with oil and place them on a foil-lined baking tray. Cover with foil and bake in a hot oven for 10 minutes.

3. While the fish is cooking, prepare the sauce. Heat the oil in a frying pan over a medium heat, add the cumin seeds and fry for a few seconds until they start to darken.

4. Add the onion and stir-fry until soft – about 5 minutes. Add the peppers, aubergines, spice powders, tomatoes and salt and give everything a good stir to coat the vegetables in the oil and spices.

5. Add the tomato purée and 4–5 tablespoons water and bring to the boil.

6. Cover with a lid, reduce the heat and simmer gently for 10 minutes.

7. To serve, place a fillet of salmon on a plate and pour some of the spicy vegetable curry over the top. Garnish with fresh coriander.

---

dinner for a Kapha imbalance (see page 11)
- salmon with a spicy vegetable curry (SABZIONWALI MACCHI)
- rice, carrot and lentil stew (GAJAR KI KHICHADI), page 21
- turmeric and jaggery tea (HALDI KI CHAI), page 161

LOBHIA AUR MACCHI

black-eyed beans with tuna

Here I have combined a bean curry with low-fat tuna steaks for a truly healthy and delicious meal. The black-eyed beans are rich in soluble fibre, which helps to lower blood cholesterol.

2 tablespoons sunflower oil
4 x 100g tuna steaks
salt, to taste
1 teaspoon cumin seeds
large pinch of asafoetida
1 medium onion, finely chopped
1 tablespoon ginger-garlic paste
 (see page 173)
1 x 400g tin black-eyed beans,
 drained and rinsed
½ teaspoon chilli powder
½ teaspoon turmeric powder
2 large ripe tomatoes,
 roughly chopped
1 teaspoon garam masala
2 celery stalks, washed and
 finely chopped
small handful fresh coriander
 leaves, washed

preparation time 10 minutes
cooking time 35 minutes
serves 4

1. Heat 1 tablespoon oil in a large frying pan over a high heat. Add the tuna steaks and seal them on one side in the hot pan. Carefully turn the steaks over and season with salt, and then reduce the heat and cover with a lid. Cook over a low heat for 7–8 minutes, or until the fish is cooked through. Take off the heat and leave to rest.

2. Heat the remaining oil in a large, heavy-based frying pan and fry the cumin seeds until they start to darken. Add the asafoetida.

3. Add the onion and fry until soft and just starting to colour – about 5 minutes – turning down the heat if they brown too quickly. Stir in the ginger-garlic paste.

4. Tip in the beans and sprinkle in the chilli powder and turmeric. Combine well.

5. Stir in the tomatoes, garam masala and celery. Season to taste with salt. Add 5–6 tablespoons water, and then cover with a lid and bring everything to the boil. Reduce the heat and simmer gently for 10 minutes.

6. When the sauce is ready, mash a few of the beans with the back of a fork to help thicken the sauce.

7. Arrange the cooked tuna steaks on top of the bean curry and replace the lid. Return the pan to a gentle heat for 2–3 minutes to allow the fish to heat through properly. Garnish with fresh coriander.

BANGDA GASSI 🐑

spicy mackerel curry

Mackerel is very popular along the western coast of India and it is widely used in fish curries. In Mumbai, you can buy mackerel within a few hours of its being caught! Oily fish such as mackerel are rich in omega-3 fatty acids that help heart health, as well as vitamin B12, which is essential for the formation of blood and for keeping the nervous system in order.

1 tablespoon coriander seeds
5 black peppercorns
1 teaspoon cumin seeds
5 dried red chillies
2 tablespoons desiccated coconut
4 tablespoons malt vinegar
4 x 125g mackerel fillets, cut in half
1 teaspoon turmeric powder
salt, to taste
2 tablespoons sunflower oil

preparation time 10 minutes
cooking time 20 minutes
serves 4

1. Put the coriander seeds, peppercorns, cumin seeds, dried red chillies, desiccated coconut, malt vinegar and 3–4 tablespoons water in a blender and blitz to a fine purée.

2. Season the fillets of mackerel with turmeric and salt.

3. Heat the oil in a heavy-based frying pan and fry the fish over a medium heat for 3–4 minutes on each side. Scoop in the mixture from the blender and top up with 150ml water to make a sauce. Season with salt.

4. Bring to the boil, and then reduce the heat and simmer gently for 8–10 minutes, or until the fish is cooked through.

LAL CHUTNEY KI MACCHI

fish baked with red coconut chutney

'Chutney fish' is an original recipe from the Zoroastrian community, who immigrated to India several hundred years ago. This dish is traditionally made with green chutney, but I think this recipe for red coconut chutney tastes delicious.

FOR THE CHUTNEY:
1 tablespoon finely grated garlic
½ teaspoon chilli powder
3 tablespoons lemon juice
salt, to taste
175g freshly grated coconut
  (or desiccated coconut)

4 x 150g white fish fillets (such
  as haddock or cod)

preparation time 15 minutes
cooking time 10 minutes
serves 4

1. Preheat your oven to 220°C/425°F/gas mark 7.

2. Place all the ingredients for the chutney in a food processor and blend to a fine paste with 3–4 tablespoons water.

3. Season each fillet of fish with a small pinch of salt. Smear with 1 heaped tablespoon of the red coconut chutney and wrap individually in foil. Place the foil parcels on a baking sheet and bake in the hot oven for 10 minutes. Alternatively, place them inside a steamer and cook for the same length of time.

SUNGTACHI AMTI

prawn curry with tamarind and tomatoes

Tamarind is a sour fruit which grows around the coastline of India. The sausage-shaped fruits ripen in May and then the pulp and seeds are processed into slabs for use all year round. Tamarind is a cooling ingredient and it is often used in summer drinks.

2 tablespoons sunflower oil
1 teaspoon coriander seeds
10 black peppercorns
2 medium onions, finely chopped
1 teaspoon finely grated garlic
2 ripe tomatoes, roughly chopped
½ teaspoon turmeric powder
½ teaspoon chilli powder
2 teaspoons tamarind paste, mixed
　　with 2–3 tablespoons water
salt, to taste
600g shelled prawns, cooked or raw
300ml coconut milk

preparation time 15 minutes
cooking time 15 minutes
serves 4

1. Heat 1 tablespoon oil in a heavy-based saucepan and fry the coriander seeds and peppercorns over a medium heat for 1 minute. Add the onions and fry until soft. Add the garlic and tomatoes and cook for a few minutes until mushy. Transfer the mixture to a blender and blitz to a smooth purée with 3–4 tablespoons water.

2. Heat the remaining tablespoon of oil in a large frying pan and fry the prawns for 1 minute over a high heat. If using raw prawns, continue cooking until they turn opaque.

3. Add the powdered spices, tamarind and salt and give everything a quick stir to coat the prawns in the oil and spices. Add 2 tablespoons water and simmer over a medium heat for 5 minutes.

4. Pour in the coconut milk, adjust the seasoning and bring to the boil. Take off the heat immediately the sauce comes to the boil to prevent the coconut milk from separating.

JHINGA JALFREZI

king prawns with green peppers, onions and tomatoes

'Jalfrezi' is a dish cooked with green peppers and onions. It has become one of the most popular recipes in restaurants around the world.

2 tablespoons sunflower oil
1 teaspoon cumin seeds
1 large onion, finely sliced
1 tablespoon ginger-garlic paste
  (see page 173)
½ teaspoon turmeric powder
½ teaspoon chilli powder
½ teaspoon ground coriander
salt, to taste
150g green peppers (stalks and seeds
  removed), sliced
300g raw, shelled king prawns
2 ripe tomatoes, sliced
handful fresh coriander leaves, washed
  and finely chopped

preparation time 10 minutes
cooking time 25 minutes
serves 4

1. Heat the oil in a heavy-based saucepan and fry the cumin seeds over a medium heat until they start to darken. Add the onion and fry until soft – about 5 minutes.

2. Add the ginger-garlic paste and stir-fry for a few seconds until well blended.

3. Sprinkle in the spice powders and salt. Cook over a low heat until the oil begins to separate – about 3 minutes – stirring frequently to prevent them from scorching.

4. Add the peppers and cook for about 8 minutes, or until they have softened slightly but still hold their shape. Add the prawns and keep stirring until they turn opaque – about 3 minutes.

5. Pour in 100ml water, bring to the boil and then simmer gently for 3–4 minutes.

6. Add the tomatoes and cook until soft but not mushy – about 2–3 minutes. Take off the heat and garnish with fresh coriander.

DARYACHI RANI 🐚

scallops baked in a coriander pesto

Scallops are rich in vitamin B12, iron, magnesium, zinc and copper. They are sold with or without their shell and should be firm, plump and sweet-smelling. Fresh scallops don't keep very well and should be eaten on the day of purchase, or stored in the fridge in an airtight container and eaten the next day. It is easy to overcook scallops, which ruins their delicate texture and toughens them.

big handful fresh coriander
1 teaspoon ginger-garlic paste
  (see page 173)
1 fresh green chilli, roughly chopped
salt, to taste
small pinch of sugar
squeeze of lemon
olive oil, for brushing
16 prepared scallops
16 scallop shells, to serve (optional)

preparation time 15 minutes
cooking time 5 minutes
serves 4

1. Preheat your oven to 190°C/375°F/gas mark 5.

2. Wash the fresh coriander and roughly chop. Place it in a small blender or coffee mill with the ginger-garlic paste and chilli and blitz to a fine paste with 3–4 tablespoons water. Scoop into a bowl and season with salt, sugar and lemon juice. Drop in the scallops and coat well.

3. Brush a baking tray or the scallop shells (if using) with olive oil and arrange the scallopson the tray or inside the shells. Spoon over any remaining pesto sauce and drizzle with olive oil. Bake in the preheated oven for 5–7 minutes and serve at once.

an elegant supper

- scallops baked in a coriander pesto (DARYACHI RANI)
- corn and coriander bread (MAKAI DHANIYE KI ROTI), page 25
- chicken and potato curry with egg drops (ALOO MURGH RASHIDA), page 54
- black lentils cooked with spices (KALI DAL), page 78
- peas with cottage cheese (MUTTER PANEER), page 92
- date and almond fudge (KHAJUR AUR BADAM KA HALWA), page 164

TISRYA KADHI

steamed coconut clams

Clams have a sweet flavour and a delicate texture. In Indian cooking, they are often combined with coconut to complement their sweetness. They are very high in iron and also contain zinc, copper, manganese and selenium.

600g fresh clams
salt, to taste
2 tablespoons sunflower oil
1 medium onion, finely chopped
3 garlic cloves, peeled and finely grated
½ teaspoon crushed black pepper
½ teaspoon turmeric powder
1 x 400ml tin coconut milk

preparation time 10 minutes
cooking time 20 minutes
serves 4

1. Wash the clams under plenty of cold, running water. Discard any that are open and refuse to close when you tap them.

2. Heat the oil in a heavy-based saucepan and fry the onion over a high heat until soft – about 5 minutes. Add the garlic, black pepper and turmeric.

3. Pour in 150ml water and bring to the boil. Add the clams, cover with a lid and steam for 9–10 minutes, stirring occasionally so that they cook evenly.

4. Take off the lid and discard any clams that are not fully open. Pour in the coconut milk and heat through.

NANDU KARI

coastal crab curry

4 tablespoons sunflower oil
8 cloves
10 black peppercorns
2 teaspoons coriander seeds
3 medium onions, finely sliced
150g freshly grated coconut
   (or desiccated coconut)
1 x 600g whole cooked crab
1 teaspoon chilli powder
1 teaspoon turmeric powder
salt, to taste
1 tablespoon tamarind paste, mixed
   with 2–3 tablespoons water
5 tablespoons coconut milk

preparation time 15 minutes
cooking time 40 minutes
serves 4

1. To prepare the crab, first twist the legs and claws until they come apart from the body. Then cut the body in half and throw away the stomach sac, mouth piece, intestines and feathery-looking gills.

2. Heat 2 tablespoons oil in a heavy-based saucepan over a medium heat. Add the cloves, peppercorns and coriander seeds and wait for them to sizzle. Now add the onion and fry over a low heat until golden – about 5 minutes.

3. Stir in the coconut and fry until brown – this browning process is really important because it gives the curry its flavour. Transfer the mixture to a blender and blitz to a fine paste with 3–4 tablespoons water.

4. Heat the remaining 2 tablespoons of oil in the same pan and add the crab pieces and powdered spices. Mix well.

5. Season with salt and pour in the tamarind. Bring to the boil, and then scoop in the mixture from the blender.

6. Cover with a lid and simmer gently for 10 minutes. Pour in the coconut milk and heat through.

lentil and bean curries

In India, where many people are vegetarian due to religious reasons, lentils and pulses provide the protein element to the daily diet. Lentils are also rich in iron and dietary fibre.

Research suggests that substituting beans, peas and lentils for foods that are high in saturated fats and refined carbohydrates can help lower the risk of cardiovascular disease. Plant protein may help protect the heart by lowering blood cholesterol levels in some people.

Indian cookery uses a wide variety of beans and lentils. When beans are split, they become more like lentils and therefore two different ingredients become available to cook with. Whole black urad beans make a chewy, rich curry, for example, whereas skinned and split urad lentils ('urad dal') result in a gloopy dish. In southern India, urad dal are made into batter for pancakes called 'dosas'.

Ayurvedic wisdom

On the whole, lentils and beans are classed as heating foods and need to be teamed with cooling ingredients to balance them (see page 13). Many traditional Ayurvedic recipes combine them with rice and vegetables for this purpose.

MASOORICHI DAL

brown lentils with onion and coconut

Brown lentils are split commercially to produce red or pink lentils, giving two completely different ingredients to cook with. This recipe uses whole brown lentils, but you can use Puy lentils or whole green lentils if you prefer. Lentils are high in fibre, calcium and iron, making them a good substitute for meat in a vegetarian diet.

300g whole brown lentils ('masoor')
  or Puy lentils, soaked overnight
2 tablespoons sunflower oil
1 teaspoon cumin seeds
2 medium red onions, finely sliced
1 green chilli, very finely chopped
2 teaspoons ginger-garlic paste
  (see page 173)
2 ripe tomatoes, finely chopped
1 teaspoon turmeric powder
salt, to taste
small handful fresh coriander leaves,
  washed and finely chopped
2 tablespoons freshly grated coconut
  (or desiccated coconut)

**preparation time 10 minutes
  (+ overnight soaking)
cooking time 45 minutes**
serves 4

1. Drain and rinse the lentils, and then place them in a saucepan with double the volume of hot water. Bring to the boil and then simmer for 35 minutes, or until the lentils are mushy.

2. Heat the oil over a high heat in a heavy-based saucepan. Add the cumin seeds and allow them to darken slightly. Add the onions and fry until soft – about 5 minutes.

3. Add the chilli and ginger-garlic paste and stir for a few seconds.

4. Drop in the tomatoes and turmeric and cook until soft and well blended.

5. Season with salt, and then pour in the cooked lentils. Stir in the fresh coriander and coconut and serve hot.

---

a warming, autumn dinner

- brown lentils with onion and coconut (MASOORICHI DAL)
- brown basmati with chicken, cinnamon and sunflower seeds
  (MURGH DALCHINI PULAO), page 22
- aubergine salad with red onion and tomatoes (DAHI BAINGAN BHARTA),
  page 144

gold mung dal

Mung beans are available either as small, dried, whole green beans or as split, yellow lentils called 'dal' (sold with or without their skins). Mung dal are highly regarded in Ayurveda because they are lighter, cooler and easier to digest than most other beans – making them an ideal ingredient in summer. Here, I have combined them with peanuts for added protein. You can leave these out if you are allergic to nuts.

150g split mung dal (with their skins on), soaked in cold water for 1 hour
50g roasted peanuts, salted or unsalted
1 tablespoon sunflower oil
pinch of asafoetida
1 medium onion, finely chopped
1 small green chilli, very finely chopped
1 teaspoon ginger-garlic paste (see page 173)
½ teaspoon turmeric powder
2 ripe tomatoes, roughly chopped
salt, to taste
small handful fresh coriander leaves, washed and finely chopped

preparation time 10 minutes (+ 1 hour soaking)
cooking time 30 minutes
serves 4

1. Wash the dal in several changes of water. Place them in a heavy-based saucepan with 300ml hot water and bring to the boil. Add the peanuts, and then reduce the heat and simmer for about 20 minutes, or until cooked.

2. Heat the oil in a heavy-based saucepan over a high heat. Add the asafoetida and onion and fry until soft – about 5 minutes.

3. Add the chilli, ginger-garlic paste, turmeric and tomatoes and stir to blend for 2–3 minutes.

4. Pour in the cooked dal, thinning with a little water for a soupy consistency. Season with salt. Serve hot, sprinkled with fresh coriander.

SHENGA-MOOLYACHI AAMTI

yellow lentils with drumsticks and mooli

Drumsticks are long, thin, green vegetables which grow on big trees in India. The inner flesh is similar in texture to a courgette.

1 small mooli, washed and cut into 1cm cubes
150g split yellow lentils ('toor dal')
2 drumsticks, cut into 6cm lengths
salt, to taste
1 tablespoon sunflower oil
½ teaspoon black mustard seeds
large pinch asafoetida
½ teaspoon cumin seeds
10 curry leaves
2 green chillies, finely sliced
½ teaspoon turmeric powder
2 ripe tomatoes, roughly chopped
juice of ½ lemon
small handful fresh coriander leaves,
  washed and roughly chopped

preparation time 10 minutes
cooking time 35 minutes
serves 4

1. Place the mooli and lentils in a saucepan and cover with double their volume of hot water. Bring to the boil, and then cover with a lid and simmer for about 30 minutes, or until soft and mushy. When cooked, the lentils should have a thick, custard-like consistency.

2. Meanwhile, place the pieces of drumstick in a small saucepan and pour over enough water to just cover them. Season with salt. Bring to the boil, and then reduce the heat, cover with a lid and simmer for 10 minutes.

3. Heat the oil in a large, heavy-based saucepan over a high heat. Add the mustard seeds. When they pop, add the asafoetida, cumin, curry leaves and chillies. Fry together for 1 minute.

4. Add the turmeric and cooked lentils, and then pour in the drumsticks along with their cooking liquid.

5. Bring everything to the boil, stirring all the time, and then add the tomatoes and salt. Cook for 2–3 minutes to soften the tomatoes, and then stir in the lemon juice and fresh coriander.

black-eyed beans in a yogurt curry

Black-eyed beans are a rich source of good-quality protein. They are low in sodium and high in potassium, and are helpful in maintaining healthy blood pressure.

2 tablespoons sunflower oil
1 teaspoon cumin seeds
large pinch asafoetida
1 medium onion, finely sliced
1 small green chilli, very finely
    chopped
1 tablespoon ginger-garlic paste
    (see page 173)
150g tinned black-eyed beans,
    rinsed and drained
½ teaspoon turmeric powder
2 teaspoons tomato purée
1 teaspoon garam masala
salt, to taste
2 tablespoons natural, low-fat
    yogurt (probiotic, if possible)
small handful fresh coriander
    leaves, washed and finely
    chopped

**preparation time 15 minutes
    (+ overnight soaking, if using
    dried beans)
cooking time 20 minutes**
serves 4

1. Heat the oil in a heavy-based saucepan over a high heat. Add the cumin seeds and fry until they start to darken.

2. Add the asafoetida and onion and stir-fry until soft and beginning to turn golden – about 5 minutes. Add the chilli and ginger-garlic paste and mix well.

3. Tip in the beans, sprinkle in the turmeric and fry together for 1 minute.

4. Add the tomato purée, garam masala and salt and stir to combine. Pour in enough water to cover the beans and bring to the boil. Reduce the heat, cover with a lid and simmer until cooked –- about 10 minutes. When cooked, the beans should still retain their shape. Mash a few of them with a fork to thicken the curry.

5. Stir in the yogurt and garnish with fresh coriander.

RAJMA ⬤ ⬤

red kidney beans with tomatoes

If you are using dried kidney beans for this recipe, first soak them overnight in cold water, and then rinse them thoroughly and boil for at least an hour in fresh water. I prefer to use tinned beans, which I always wash and drain well to get rid of any salt.

1 x 400g tin chopped tomatoes
1 tablespoon sunflower oil
½ teaspoon ginger-garlic paste
   (see page 173)
½ teaspoon turmeric powder
½ teaspoon chilli powder
1 teaspoon ground coriander
1 x 400g tin red kidney beans,
   drained and rinsed
salt, to taste
handful fresh coriander leaves,
   washed and finely chopped

preparation time 5 minutes
cooking time 15 minutes
serves 4

1. Blitz the tinned tomatoes in a blender to make a smooth purée.

2. Heat the oil in a heavy-based saucepan and add the ginger-garlic paste. Add the spice powders and give them a quick stir to stop them from scorching.

3. Tip in the tomato purée from the blender and cook for 2–3 minutes over a high heat until well blended. Stir in the beans and season with salt.

4. Reduce the heat and simmer gently for 5–7 minutes. Serve hot, sprinkled with fresh coriander.

---

dinner for a Pitta imbalance (see page 10)

- red kidney beans with tomatoes (RAJMA)
- plain boiled rice (CHAVAL), page 18
- ivy gourds with coconut (TENDLI UPKARI), page 115
- cucumber and mint raita (KHEERE PUDINA KA RAITA), page 136

mung bean and coconut curry

Indian cooking has always included sprouting of beans and pulses. The sprouting process reduces calories and carbohydrates and increases the vitamin, mineral and protein content. Mung sprouts have a higher content of vitamin C and iron than beans that are not sprouted. In Ayurveda, mung sprouts are classed as cooling and are best suited to people with a Pitta constitution.

300g mung beans
1 teaspoon turmeric powder
salt, to taste
2 tablespoons sunflower oil
1 teaspoon coriander seeds
4 dried red chillies (stalks and
   seeds removed), crumbled
150g freshly grated coconut
   (or desiccated coconut)
1 teaspoon tamarind paste, mixed
   with 2 tablespoons water
1 medium onion, finely chopped

preparation time 20 minutes
   (+ overnight soaking + 8 hours
   sprouting)
cooking time 30 minutes
serves 4

1. Soak the beans overnight in cold water, and then rinse them thoroughly in fresh water and place them in a sieve to drain. Leave them in a warm place to sprout for 8 hours – for example, near a radiator or in the airing cupboard.

2. Place the sprouted beans in a saucepan with enough water to cover them. Add the turmeric and salt. Bring to the boil, and then reduce the heat and simmer for 12–15 minutes, or until the beans are cooked. They should absorb most of the cooking liquid.

3. Meanwhile, heat 1 tablespoon oil in a heavy-based saucepan and fry the coriander seeds and chillies until they start to darken. Add the coconut and tamarind.

4. Transfer this mixture to a blender and blitz to a smooth purée with a few tablespoons water.

5. Heat the remaining oil in a frying pan and fry the onion for 5 minutes until soft.

6. Tip the onions into the pan of cooked mung beans, scoop in the coconut and tamarind purée and heat through.

black lentils cooked with spices

Whole black lentils are considered to be heavy for the digestion, which is why I've combined them here with digestive spices, such as asafoetida, and ingredients such as ginger and garlic that stimulate 'agni' and help the digestive process.

2 tablespoons sunflower oil
1 large onion, finely chopped
1 tablespoon ginger-garlic paste
  (see page 173)
large pinch asafoetida
1 teaspoon turmeric powder
1 teaspoon chilli powder
1 teaspoon garam masala
2 large tomatoes, roughly chopped
150g whole black lentils, soaked
  overnight
salt, to taste
3–4 tablespoons dried red kidney
  beans, soaked overnight and then
  boiled for at least an hour
2 tablespoons finely chopped fresh
  coriander leaves

**preparation time 15 minutes
  (+ overnight soaking)
cooking time 1 hour 15 minutes**
serves 4

1. Heat the oil in a large, heavy-based saucepan and fry the onion over a high heat until soft – about 5 minutes. Add the ginger-garlic paste and asafoetida.

2. Stir in the spice powders and tomatoes and cook for a few minutes to blend.

3. Drain and rinse the black lentils and add them to the pan with the salt. Pour in 300ml hot water and bring to the boil. Reduce the heat and simmer for about an hour, or until the lentils are cooked. Mash a few of the lentils with a fork to thicken the curry.

4. Add the red kidney beans and simmer for 5 minutes. Garnish with fresh coriander.

METHI DAL

lentils with tomato and fenugreek seeds

Fenugreek seeds are slightly square in shape and mustard yellow in colour. They have a bitter 'rasa' or taste, and are therefore helpful in cleansing the body of toxins. In India, they are often given to lactating mothers because they are thought to increase the production of breast milk. They are widely used in Ayurveda for weight loss and cleansing therapies. A daily cup of fenugreek tea is said to be revitalising.

220g split red lentils, washed and drained
2 tablespoons sunflower oil
1 teaspoon black mustard seeds
½ teaspoon fenugreek seeds
large pinch asafoetida
12 curry leaves
4 dried red chillies (stalks and seeds removed)
1 teaspoon turmeric powder
3 ripe tomatoes, roughly chopped
salt, to taste
small handful fresh coriander leaves, washed and finely chopped

preparation time 5 minutes
cooking time 35 minutes
serves 4

1. Place the lentils in a saucepan with double their volume of water. Bring to the boil, cover and simmer for about 25 minutes, or until soft.

2. Heat the oil in a heavy-based saucepan over a high heat. Add the mustard seeds and wait for them to pop, and then add the fenugreek seeds, asafoetida, curry leaves and red chillies. Fry for a few seconds until the fenugreek seeds darken slightly.

3. Add the turmeric and tomatoes, season with salt and cook for 3–4 minutes until the tomatoes soften.

4. Pour in the cooked lentils, adding a little extra water to give the consistency of thick soup. Stir in the fresh coriander, adjust the seasoning and serve hot.

lentils with wholewheat dumplings

This curry is flavoured with jaggery, a form of concentrated sugar cane which is used in many Indian recipes as a substitute for refined sugar. According to the ancient medical text *Sushruta Samhita*, jaggery is helpful in purifying the blood and treating rheumatic conditions.

220g split yellow lentils ('toor dal'), washed and drained
1 tablespoon sunflower oil
1 teaspoon black mustard seeds
½ teaspoon fenugreek seeds
10 curry leaves
½ teaspoon chilli powder
½ teaspoon turmeric powder
1 teaspoon ground cumin
1 teaspoon ground coriander
salt, to taste
1 teaspoon tamarind paste, mixed with 2–3 tablespoons water
1 teaspoon jaggery (or soft brown sugar)

FOR THE DUMPLINGS:
150g wholewheat flour ('atta'), available from Indian grocers
½ teaspoon turmeric powder
½ teaspoon chilli powder
salt, to taste

preparation time 25 minutes
cooking time 45 minutes
serves 4

1. Place the lentils in a saucepan with double their volume of water and bring to the boil. Reduce the heat, cover and simmer for 30 minutes until the lentils are soft and mushy.

2. Meanwhile, combine the ingredients for the dumplings in a mixing bowl and mix to a soft dough with a little water. Knead well until the mixture is no longer sticky. Divide the dough into 10 balls.

3. Heat the oil over a high heat in a heavy-based saucepan and add the mustard and fenugreek seeds. As soon as they pop and darken, add the curry leaves, powdered spices, salt, tamarind and jaggery (or sugar).

4. Pour in the cooked lentils and bring to the boil.

5. Roll out each ball of dough into a flat disc, 5mm thick, and cut into diamond shapes with a sharp knife.

6. Once the lentils have come to the boil, add the wheat flour dumplings to the pan and let them cook for 3–4 minutes until soft.

CHANNA MASALEDAR

spicy chickpeas

A tin of chickpeas is one of the most versatile ingredients in my kitchen cupboard. They are high in protein and can be easily spiced and combined with a salad and some couscous for a quick, healthy meal. I also make a dip with them – similar to hummus, but spiced with chilli and garlic.

2 tablespoons sunflower oil
2 medium onions, finely sliced
1 tablespoon ginger-garlic paste
  (see page 173)
2 tablespoons tomato purée
1 teaspoon turmeric powder
½ teaspoon chilli powder
1 teaspoon ground coriander
1 teaspoon ground cumin
1 x 400g tin chickpeas, drained
  and rinsed
salt, to taste

preparation time 15 minutes
cooking time 15 minutes
serves 4

1. Heat 1 tablespoon oil in a heavy-based saucepan and fry the onions over a high heat until soft.

2. Add the ginger-garlic paste and tomato purée and fry until mushy.

3. Cool slightly, and then transfer the mixture to a blender and blitz to a smooth purée with a few tablespoons water. This is the curry paste.

4. Rinse out the pan and use it to heat the remaining tablespoon of oil. Add the powdered spices and chickpeas – do this at once or the spices will scorch in the hot oil.

5. Spoon in the curry paste, season with salt and mix well.

6. Pour in 150ml water and bring to the boil. Reduce the heat and simmer for 5 minutes until the curry is well blended.

vegetable curries

It is easy to be vegetarian in India because of the vast variety of vegetables available. From gourds such as 'karela' (bitter gourd) and 'tindora' (ivy gourd) to okra, aubergines and pumpkins, there is possibly a different vegetable for every day of the month!

Many vegetables contain powerful antioxidants, such as vitamin C, which help the body restore itself to health after periods of stress or illness. Vegetables also contain valuable fibre to keep the digestion running smoothly.

Ayurvedic wisdom

Most vegetables are classed as moist, nourishing and easy to digest if cooked and seasoned appropriately. Different vegetables affect the body in different ways, depending on their nature. Warming vegetables, including aubergine or beetroot, are most advantageous to Vata and Kapha; cooling vegetables, such as cabbage or cauliflower, are better suited to Pitta.

BHOPLYACHI BHAJI

sweet and sour pumpkin curry

Pumpkin is rich in fibre and cancer-fighting antioxidants. It is very high in vitamin A, which keeps the eyesight in order and strengthens the immune system. I tend to leave the skin on when cooking pumpkin – not only is this healthier, but the skin tastes wonderful and helps the pumpkin retain its shape.

2 tablespoons sunflower oil
3 dried red chillies (seeds removed)
½ teaspoon cumin seeds
6 black peppercorns
1 teaspoon white poppy seeds
½ teaspoon fenugreek seeds
5 tablespoons freshly grated coconut
   (or desiccated coconut)
½ teaspoon black mustard seeds
300g pumpkin, washed and cut
   into 2.5cm cubes
1 tablespoon tamarind paste, mixed
   with 6 tablespoons water
1 tablespoon jaggery (or soft
   brown sugar)
salt, to taste

preparation time 15 minutes
cooking time 40 minutes
serves 4

1. Heat 1 tablespoon oil in a heavy-based saucepan and fry the chillies, cumin seeds, peppercorns, poppy seeds and fenugreek seeds over a high heat until they start to colour.

2. Reduce the heat, add the coconut and fry until golden brown. Cool slightly, and then transfer the mixture to a blender and blitz to a fine paste with a few tablespoons water.

3. Wipe out the pan and use it to heat the remaining tablespoon of oil over a high heat. Add the mustard seeds and wait for them to pop. Now add the pumpkin cubes and turn them in the hot oil.

4. Pour in the tamarind and add the jaggery (or sugar) and salt.

5. Spoon in the mixture from the blender and bring to the boil, and then reduce the heat and simmer for 12–15 minutes until the pumpkin is tender.

DOODHI CHANNA ◉ ◉

bottle gourd with lentils

Bottle gourd ('doodhi') is valued in Ayurveda as a cooling, diuretic vegetable that is helpful in soothing urinary disorders. It is alkaline in nature and can relieve acidity and ulcers.

3 tablespoons split yellow gram lentils ('chana dal'), washed
1 medium bottle gourd (or courgette)
2 tablespoons sunflower oil
1 teaspoon cumin seeds
pinch of asafoetida
½ teaspoon turmeric powder
salt, to taste
1 teaspoon ground coriander
2.5cm piece fresh root ginger, scraped and grated
1 ripe tomato, roughly chopped
handful fresh coriander leaves, washed and finely chopped

preparation time 10 minutes
cooking time 30 minutes
serves 4

1. Soak the gram lentils in a little water while you peel the bottle gourd (or courgette) and cut it into 1cm cubes.

2. Heat a heavy-based saucepan and add the oil. Fry the cumin seeds over a high heat until they start to darken, and then add the asafoetida and turmeric. Drain the lentils and add them to the pan with 150ml water. Bring to the boil, and then reduce heat and simmer until soft – about 10 minutes.

3. Add the bottle gourd (or courgette), salt, ground coriander, ginger and tomato and mix well. Bring everything to the boil, adding more water if necessary to prevent the curry from drying out.

4. Reduce the heat, cover and simmer for 15 minutes. Garnish with fresh coriander.

GUCCHI METHI ALOO

fresh fenugreek with potatoes and mushrooms

Fenugreek seeds are used as a spice, whereas the leaves are used as a vegetable. Both have a curry-like aroma and a slightly bitter taste which is valued in Ayurvedic detoxification therapies.

1 bunch fresh fenugreek leaves ('methi') – these are available from Indian grocers in conveniently tied bunches
1 tablespoon sunflower oil
½ teaspoon cumin seeds
2 medium onions, finely sliced
2 large potatoes, washed and cut into 2cm cubes
¼ teaspoon chilli powder
1 teaspoon ground coriander
2 large tomatoes, roughly chopped
handful closed cup mushrooms, washed and sliced
salt, to taste

preparation time 15 minutes
cooking time 25 minutes
serves 4

1. Pinch the leaves off the fenugreek, discarding the thick, central stalks. Wash, drain and chop the leaves.

2. Heat the oil in a heavy-based saucepan and fry the cumin seeds over a high heat until they start to darken. Add the onions and cook until soft – about 5 minutes.

3. Add the potatoes and turn them in the pan to coat them in the hot oil and spices. Add the fenugreek and stir-fry until the leaves are wilted.

4. Add the rest of the ingredients along with 100ml water. Bring to the boil, and then cover and simmer over a low heat for 15 minutes until the potatoes are tender.

KHUMB KORMA 🔥 🔥

mildly spiced mushroom curry

Mushrooms are classed as 'tamasic' in Ayurveda – that is, belonging to a group of foods including alcohol and meat that promote lethargy and resistance, so they are best eaten in moderation.

1 large onion, finely sliced
1 fresh green chilli, finely chopped
50g cashew nuts
2 tablespoons sunflower oil
2 teaspoons ginger-garlic paste
   (see page 173)
300g mushrooms, sliced
salt, to taste
1 teaspoon ground coriander
1 teaspoon ground cumin
½ teaspoon garam masala

preparation time 10 minutes
cooking time 25 minutes
serves 4

1. Place the onion, chilli and cashew nuts in a small saucepan, adding enough water to cover. Bring to the boil, and then simmer for about 10 minutes, or until the onions are soft. Transfer to a blender and blitz to a smooth paste.

2. Heat the oil in a heavy-based saucepan over a high heat. Add the ginger-garlic paste, followed by the mushrooms.

3. Season with salt and sprinkle in the ground coriander and cumin. Give everything a quick stir to coat the mushrooms in the spices, and then spoon in the mixture from the blender.

4. Bring to the boil, stirring all the time, and then simmer for 10 minutes until the mushrooms are tender.

5. To finish, sprinkle over the garam masala.

BAINGAN CHOLAY MASALA

aubergine and chickpea curry

Indian cooking uses two kinds of chickpeas – a small, dark variety and the larger, light-coloured one that we are familiar with in the West. Chickpeas are rich in carbohydrates, protein and zinc.

2 tablespoons sunflower oil
2 medium onions, finely sliced
2 teaspoons ginger-garlic paste
(see page 173)
2 tablespoons tomato purée
1 green chilli, finely chopped
1 medium aubergine, cut into
2.5cm cubes
1 teaspoon turmeric powder
1 teaspoon ground coriander
salt, to taste
200g tinned chickpeas, drained
and rinsed
2 tablespoons finely chopped fresh
coriander leaves, plus extra to
garnish

preparation time 10 minutes
cooking time 30 minutes
serves 4

1. Heat 1 tablespoon oil in a heavy-based saucepan and fry the onions over a high heat until soft – about 5 minutes.

2. Add the ginger-garlic paste and tomato purée and fry until mushy. Add the chilli.

3. Cool slightly, and then transfer the mixture to a blender and blitz to a smooth purée with a few tablespoons water, if necessary.

4. Wipe out the pan and use it to heat the remaining tablespoon of oil. Add the aubergine and powdered spices and stir-fry for 1 minute to coat the aubergine in the oil and spices.

5. Add the mixture from the blender and season with salt.

6. Pour in 100ml water and bring to the boil, stirring all the time.

7. Add the chickpeas, and then reduce the heat, cover with a lid and cook for about 15 minutes, or until the aubergine is tender.

8. Garnish with fresh coriander.

MAKKAI PALAK

spinach and sweetcorn curry

Spinach is a commonly used ingredient all over India. It is classed as a cooling, soothing vegetable in Ayurveda, which is why I have balanced it with warming spices to kindle the body's digestive fire. We all know that spinach is packed with iron, but it also contains oxalic acid, which inhibits the absorption of iron by the body. To remedy this, combine it with animal protein or vegetables that are rich in vitamin C (such as tomatoes, broccoli or potatoes).

450g fresh spinach, washed and drained
2 tablespoons sunflower oil
½ teaspoon cumin seeds
2.5cm piece fresh root ginger, scraped and finely grated
2 large tomatoes, roughly chopped
4 tablespoons sweetcorn (frozen or tinned)
½ teaspoon chilli powder
½ teaspoon garam masala
salt, to taste

preparation time 10 minutes
cooking time 25 minutes
serves 4

1. Place the spinach in a heavy-based saucepan and cook over a high heat until it wilts – about 5 minutes. Allow to cool slightly, and then transfer to a blender and blitz to a thick purée with any of the cooking juices.

2. Heat the oil in a heavy-based saucepan and fry the cumin seeds over a high heat until they start to darken.

3. Add the grated ginger and tomatoes and stir for 2–3 minutes until mushy.

4. Add the sweetcorn, chilli and garam masala and season to taste with salt. Add 5–6 tablespoons water and bring to the boil. Reduce the heat and simmer gently for 5 minutes until the sweetcorn is cooked.

5. Stir in the puréed spinach and heat through.

BHINDI KADHI

okra and gram flour curry

Gram flour ('besan') is a versatile ingredient used all over India. It is the essential ingredient in onion bhajias and is used as a thickener in many curries. Gram flour is made from ground yellow gram lentils ('chana dal'). It is high in carbohydrates but free from gluten, making it ideal for those with a gluten allergy.

2 tablespoons sunflower oil
½ teaspoon fenugreek seeds
3–4 curry leaves
1 teaspoon finely grated fresh root
    ginger, plus extra for garnishing
2 medium potatoes, washed and
    cut into 2cm cubes
½ teaspoon turmeric powder
½ teaspoon chilli powder
300g okra, washed, dried and
    cut in half lengthways
2 tablespoons gram flour, dry-
    roasted over a low heat for 7–8
    minutes to intensify the flavour
2 tablespoons tomato purée
1 teaspoon tamarind paste
salt, to taste

preparation time 15 minutes
cooking time 30 minutes
serves 4

1. Heat the oil in a heavy-based saucepan and add the fenugreek seeds and curry leaves. Allow them to darken over a medium heat, and then stir in the ginger.

2. Add the potatoes and powdered spices. Pour in 5 –6 tablespoons water and cook for 7–8 minutes, or until the potatoes are half-done. Add the okra and stir to combine.

3. In a separate bowl, combine the gram flour, tomato purée and tamarind with a little water to make a smooth paste. Add this mixture to the vegetables. Pour in 300ml water and bring to the boil, stirring all the time to prevent the gram flour from sticking. Season with salt. Reduce the heat and simmer for about 12 minutes, or until the potatoes and okra are tender and the curry is thick. Garnish with finely shredded ginger.

CHUKANDAR KI SUBZI

beetroot with red kidney beans

Ayurveda classes beetroot as warm, sweet and moist, and it will improve a lazy digestion because of its fibre content. This soluble fibre will also help to reduce high blood cholesterol levels. Beetroot is very rich in folate, which can protect against high blood pressure and Alzheimer's.

1 x 400g tin red kidney beans,
   drained and rinsed
1 tablespoon sunflower oil
½ teaspoon mustard seeds
¼ teaspoon cumin seeds
pinch of asafoetida
5 curry leaves
½ teaspoon chilli powder
½ teaspoon ground coriander
4 cooked beetroots, cut into
   2cm cubes
3 tablespoons finely chopped
   fresh coriander leaves
1 tablespoon desiccated coconut

preparation time 10 minutes
cooking time 15 minutes
serves 4

1. Tip half the kidney beans into a bowl and mash them with a fork. The rest can be kept whole.

2. Heat the oil in a heavy-based saucepan over a high heat and fry the mustard seeds until they pop. Add the cumin seeds, asafoetida and curry leaves.

3. Tip in the mashed and whole kidney beans and pour in 150ml water. Bring to the boil, stirring all the time.

4. Sprinkle in the powdered spices, and then carefully stir in the beetroot, fresh coriander and coconut. Simmer for 2–3 minutes.

MUTTER PANEER

peas with cottage cheese

Indian cottage cheese, known as paneer, is wonderfully cooling for Pitta, and for Vata who find its moist heaviness balancing. It is too heavy for Kapha to eat regularly, but is certainly easier for them to digest than many hard cheeses. Paneer is available from Indian grocers and some supermarkets, or you can make your own (see page 173).

2 medium onions, roughly chopped
2 tablespoons sunflower oil
2 teaspoons ginger-garlic paste
  (see page 173)
2 tablespoons tomato purée
salt, to taste
½ teaspoon chilli powder
1 teaspoon turmeric powder
1 teaspoon ground cumin
300g frozen peas
150g paneer, cut into 2.5cm cubes

preparation time 10 minutes
cooking time 25 minutes
serves 4

1. Place the onions in a small saucepan with enough water just to cover them. Bring to the boil, and then reduce the heat and simmer until soft and translucent. Transfer them, along with their cooking liquid, to a blender and blitz to a smooth paste.

2. Heat the oil in a heavy-based saucepan and fry the ginger-garlic paste for 1 minute over a high heat.

3. Spoon in the mixture from the blender and cook for 2–3 minutes, stirring. Add the tomato purée, salt and spices.

4. Add the peas and pour in 100ml water. Bring to the boil, and then reduce the heat and simmer for 5 minutes.

5. Scatter the cubes of paneer over the top and simmer for 1 minute to soften them.

FARASBEAN BHAJI

green beans in a tomato curry

Green beans are accepted by all the doshas. They are packed with dietary fibre, and are an excellent source of vitamins A, C and K, which is so vital in maintaining healthy bones.

2 tablespoons sunflower oil
1 teaspoon black mustard seeds
1 teaspoon cumin seeds
large pinch asafoetida
1 large onion, finely chopped
300g green beans, cut into
  2cm lengths
½ teaspoon turmeric powder
½ teaspoon chilli powder
1 teaspoon ground coriander
salt, to taste
1 x 400g tin chopped tomatoes
2 tablespoons cashew nuts

preparation time 15 minutes
cooking time 25 minutes
serves 4

1. Heat the oil in a heavy-based saucepan over a high heat and add the mustard seeds. When they pop, add the cumin seeds and asafoetida. Allow the cumin to darken, and then add the onion. Cook for 5 minutes until soft.

2. Add the green beans, powdered spices and salt.

3. Pour in the tomatoes and bring up to the boil, and then reduce the heat and simmer for 10 minutes until the beans are cooked. Add the cashew nuts and take off the heat.

FLOWERCHA RASSA

cauliflower with coconut and pepper

Ayurveda classes cauliflower as cold and heavy, and it is therefore best suited to Pitta and Kapha. Vata should avoid it, although cooking it with spices makes it a bit easier to handle.

Storing a cauliflower on its stem will help to reduce the brown spots that appear on the florets due to moisture.

2 tablespoons sunflower oil
10 peppercorns
5 cloves
1 tablespoon coriander seeds
1 medium onion, finely chopped
150g freshly grated coconut
  (or desiccated coconut)
450g cauliflower, cut into florets
1 teaspoon turmeric powder
½ teaspoon chilli powder
2 large tomatoes, roughly chopped
salt, to taste

preparation time 15 minutes
cooking time 25 minutes
serves 4

1. Heat 1 tablespoon oil in a heavy-based saucepan and fry the peppercorns, cloves and coriander seeds for 1 minute over a high heat to release their flavour.

2. Add the onion and stir until well browned. Add the coconut and allow it to colour also. Take off the heat and leave to cool slightly, and then transfer to a blender and blitz to a smooth paste with a few tablespoons water.

3. Wipe out the pan and use it to heat the remaining tablespoon of oil over a high heat. Add the cauliflower and stir-fry in the hot oil for a couple of minutes. Add the spice powders, tomatoes and salt and cook together for 5 minutes until the tomatoes are mushy and well blended.

4. Spoon in the mixture from the blender and top up with 150ml hot water. Bring to the boil, and then reduce the heat and simmer for 10–12 minutes, or until the cauliflower is just soft enough to pierce with a knife.

---

a vegetarian Christmas dinner

- cauliflower with coconut and pepper (FLOWERCHA RASSA)
- spring onions with gram flour (KANDYACHA ZUNKA), page 110
- broken wheat flavoured with tomato (TOMATOCHI LAPSI), page 19
- broad beans with black salt and coriander (SEIM PHALLI KA CHAAT), page 141
- sweet tamarind and vegetable chutney (MEETHI IMLI KI CHUTNEY), page 149
- lentil pudding with jaggery (MADGANE), page 167

HIRVYA FLOWERCHE SUKKE

broccoli and tamarind curry

Jaggery is not easily available outside India, so you might have to substitute it with brown sugar. For variety, you might like to use cauliflower or peas instead of broccoli, both of which go well with the fruity tartness of the tamarind.

2 tablespoons sunflower oil
1 teaspoon split black lentils ('urad dal')
1 teaspoon coriander seeds
5 dried red chillies
4 tablespoons freshly grated coconut (or desiccated coconut)
1 teaspoon tamarind paste, mixed with 6 tablespoons water
½ teaspoon turmeric powder
300g broccoli, cut into florets
salt, to taste
½ teaspoon jaggery (or soft brown sugar)

preparation time 15 minutes
cooking time 30 minutes
serves 4

1. Heat 1 tablespoon oil in a heavy-based saucepan and fry the lentils, coriander seeds and chillies until they start to change colour.

2. Add the coconut and fry until brown, stirring to prevent it from sticking. Take off the heat and cool slightly. Transfer the mixture to a blender and blitz to a smooth purée with the tamarind juice and a few tablespoons water. The final mixture should be the same consistency as pouring cream. Stir in the turmeric.

3. Heat the remaining tablespoon oil over a high heat in a kadhai (or heavy-based saucepan) and add the broccoli. Season with salt and jaggery (or sugar), and then pour in the blended mixture.

4. Bring to the boil, stirring, and then reduce the heat and cook for 8–9 minutes until the broccoli is tender.

egg curries

Eggs are a very rich source of protein and nutrients such as iron, phosphorous and zinc. They contain vitamin D, which is important for the absorption of calcium and is vital to bone health.

In India, eggs are a cheap source of complete protein and there are countless street stalls selling boiled eggs with chilli and salt. People stop by at any time of the day to have them as a snack.

Ayurvedic wisdom

Eggs are classed as astringent and heavy with a sweet, heating effect. They seem to increase Pitta and Kapha, but reduce Vata.

eggs and mushrooms in a coconut curry

Dry-roasting spices such as cumin seeds enhances their flavour and makes them easier to grind. Simply heat them in a small pan without any oil and wait for them to darken slightly and give off their wonderful aroma.

1 tablespoon coriander seeds

4 cloves

½ teaspoon cardamom seeds (taken from 6 cardamom pods)

4 tablespoons desiccated coconut

2 tablespoons sunflower oil

1 teaspoon mustard seeds

10 curry leaves

3 dried red chillies (stalks and seeds removed)

salt, to taste

300ml coconut milk

300g closed cup mushrooms, washed and thickly sliced

4 eggs, hard-boiled for 10–12 minutes, peeled and cut in half

preparation time 15 minutes
cooking time 15 minutes
serves 4

1. Heat a small frying pan and dry-roast the coriander seeds, cloves and cardamom seeds over a medium heat until they start to darken. Add the coconut and stir-fry for 2–3 minutes. Reduce the heat and cook until the coconut turns a rich golden brown. Transfer the mixture to a blender and blitz to a smooth paste with a few tablespoons water.

2. Heat the oil in a heavy-based saucepan over a high heat and add the mustard seeds. As they pop, add the curry leaves, chillies and salt. Scoop in the mixture from the blender, pour in the coconut milk and add the mushrooms.

3. Bring to the boil, stirring all the time, and then reduce the heat and arrange the eggs in the pan. Simmer for 1 minute, or until the eggs are heated through, and serve immediately.

BAIDA RATAN CURRY

fruity egg curry

Eggs can be difficult to digest, which is why I have combined them with cooling pineapple. Sweet pineapples are classed as 'tridoshic' in Ayurveda – that is, suitable for all the doshas (although they can aggravate Kapha if eaten in excess). Look out for Hunza apricots for this dish, which have not been treated with sulphur dioxide to enhance their colour.

2 tablespoons sunflower oil
1 large onion, finely sliced
1 tablespoon ginger-garlic paste
  (see page 173)
1 teaspoon poppy seeds
2 green chillies, finely chopped
handful mint leaves
½ teaspoon cumin seeds
2 ripe tomatoes, roughly chopped
1 teaspoon turmeric powder
1 teaspoon garam masala
8 eggs, hard-boiled for 10–12
  minutes, peeled and cut in half
salt, to taste
300ml coconut milk
2 large rings fresh pineapple,
  cut into 1cm chunks
8 dried apricots, roughly chopped

preparation time 15 minutes
cooking time 25 minutes
serves 4

1. Heat 1 tablespoon oil in a heavy-based saucepan and fry the onion for 5 minutes over a high heat until soft. Add the ginger-garlic paste, poppy seeds and chillies. Fry for 1 minute.

2. Take off the heat, cool slightly, and then transfer the mixture to a blender. Add the mint leaves and blitz to a smooth paste with 3–4 tablespoons water.

3. Heat the remaining tablespoon of oil in a heavy-based saucepan over a high heat. Add the cumin seeds and allow them to darken, and then add the tomatoes and spice powders. Keep stirring until the tomatoes begin to soften.

4. Add the mixture from the blender, arrange the eggs in the pan and season with salt. Pour in the coconut milk and bring to the boil, and then the reduce heat and simmer for 1 minute. Take off the heat and scatter with the pineapple and apricot chunks.

BAIDA PALAK CURRY

egg and spinach curry

Egg curry is a favourite on café menus in India. Here, I have made it with fresh spinach to give it a creamy texture and fresh colour. You will need hard-boiled eggs for this recipe – that is, ones that have been boiled on a high heat for 10–12 minutes.

300g spinach, washed, drained
  and chopped
2 tablespoons sunflower oil
½ teaspoon cumin seeds
2 medium onions, finely chopped
1 tablespoon ginger-garlic paste
  (see page 173)
2 tablespoons tomato purée
½ teaspoon turmeric powder
½ teaspoon chilli powder
1 teaspoon garam masala
salt, to taste
8 large, free-range eggs, hard-boiled
  for 10–12 minutes, peeled and cut
  in half

preparation time 15 minutes
cooking time 30 minutes
serves 4

1. Place the spinach in a saucepan and cook it until it has wilted.

2. Heat the oil in a heavy-based saucepan over a high heat and add the cumin seeds. As they darken, add the onions and fry until soft – about 5 minutes.

3. Add the ginger-garlic paste and tomato purée and stir. Add the spices and salt. Cook for 5–6 minutes, turning the heat down when the mixture begins to stick to the pan.

4. Stir in the spinach, along with its cooking liquid, and simmer for 5 minutes.

5. Gently place the eggs in the curry and heat through.

ANDE KI BHURJI

spicy scrambled eggs

This is the Indian version of scrambled eggs. The spices and chillies add a kick, whereas the onions and tomatoes bring a hint of sweetness. I have added pumpkin seeds for texture. These are rich in phytosterols, naturally occurring compounds that help to lower blood cholesterol levels. This dish goes well with the spinach roti on page 28.

6 large eggs
salt and pepper, to taste
2 tablespoons sunflower oil
½ teaspoon cumin seeds
1 small onion, finely chopped
2 green chillies, finely chopped
2 ripe tomatoes, roughly chopped
handful fresh coriander leaves,
   washed and finely chopped
2 teaspoons pumpkin seeds

preparation time 10 minutes
cooking time 15 minutes
serves 4

1. Beat the eggs in a large bowl and season with salt and pepper.

2. Heat the oil in a heavy-based saucepan over a high heat and fry the cumin seeds until they start to darken.

3. Add the onions and cook until soft – about 5 minutes. Add the chillies.

4. Stir in the tomatoes and fresh coriander and cook until well blended – about 3 minutes.

5. Pour in the beaten eggs and cook over a low heat, stirring all the time to scramble them. Once they are nearly set, take the eggs off the heat and continue stirring until they are soft and glossy. Serve hot, sprinkled with the pumpkin seeds.

Indian Sunday brunch

- spicy scrambled eggs (ANDE KI BHURJI)
- gram flour pancakes (BESAN KI ROTI), page 32
- spiced digestive tea (MASALA CHAI), page 160

three
vegetable side dishes

No meal in India is complete without some form of vegetable side dish. This is usually a dry or semi-dry dish called a 'subji' or 'bhaji' (nothing to do with the fried onion fritters sold in the West – the name for these is 'bhajia'). Vegetable side dishes provide additional nutrition, as well as making a meal more interesting in colour and texture.

In northern India, subjis might contain a combination of onion, tomatoes, ginger and garlic, whereas in the south they would be sprinkled with coconut and flavoured with black mustard seeds, curry leaves and red chillies.

For many Indians, a packed lunch for work or school is a few rotis or freshly made unleavened bread with a vegetable subji, all packed into small boxes at the start of the day.

Leftover subjis have a whole range of different uses – they can be used as stuffings in pancakes or mashed up to make vegetable cakes that can be grilled or shallow fried.

Ayurvedic wisdom

Vegetables have a whole range of tastes ('rasas') including sweet, bitter, astringent and hot. These are all beneficial to the body and, for an Indian meal to be successful, it is important to include as many of these tastes as possible (see page 12).

sweet potatoes with garlic and sunflower seeds

Sweet potatoes are high in vitamin A, in the form of beta-carotene, and in vitamin C – both of which are powerful antioxidants. When buying sweet potatoes, choose firm, unbruised ones and store them in a cool, dark place to use within a week of purchase.

2 large sweet potatoes, washed and cut into 3cm thick slices
2 garlic cloves, peeled and finely grated
1 teaspoon lemon juice
1 teaspoon finely chopped fresh coriander leaves
salt, to taste
1 teaspoon sunflower oil
1 teaspoon sunflower seeds

preparation time 10 minutes
cooking time 20 minutes
serves 4

1. Preheat your oven to 220°C/425°F/gas mark 7. Line a baking tray with foil and arrange the slices of sweet potato inside.

2. Season with garlic, lemon juice, fresh coriander and salt. Drizzle a little oil over the top and cover loosely with foil, leaving the sides unsealed to allow any steam to escape.

3. Bake in the oven for 15 minutes, and then remove the foil, sprinkle with sunflower seeds and cook for a further 5 minutes to brown the potatoes.

PEELI GOBHI

cauliflower with turmeric

Turmeric is India's wonder spice and it has long been known for its antiseptic and anti-inflammatory properties. When combined with cauliflower, turmeric is said to help prevent prostate cancer. It is also a liver detoxifier. It can be added to any recipe without necessarily adding too much flavour – I even add a pinch to my bolognese sauce!

2 tablespoons sunflower oil
1 teaspoon black mustard seeds
large pinch asafoetida
8–10 curry leaves
1 green chilli, finely chopped
1 teaspoon turmeric powder
300g cauliflower, cut into florets
salt, to taste

preparation time 10 minutes
cooking time 25 minutes
serves 4

1. Heat the oil in a heavy-based saucepan over a high heat. Add the mustard seeds and wait for them to pop, and then stir in the asafoetida, curry leaves and chilli.

2. Add the turmeric and cauliflower and season with salt. Give everything a good stir to coat the cauliflower in the oil and spices, and then add 4–5 tablespoons water.

3. Cover and cook over a high heat until the water comes to the boil. Reduce the heat and simmer for 10 minutes, covered, until the cauliflower softens but still retains a slight crunch.

a warming, winter supper

- cauliflower with turmeric (PEELI GOBHI)
- lamb and aubergine curry with almonds (BADAMI BAINGAN GOSHT), page 38
- broken wheat flavoured with tomato (TOMATOCHI LAPSI), page 19
- spinach and garlic raita (PALAK KA RAITA), page 140

BAINGAN MOONGPHALI BHARTA

aubergine mash with peanuts

I like to smoke my aubergines over a gas flame for this dish to intensify their flavour; however, doing them under a grill also works fine. First wash and dry the aubergines, and then place them directly over the gas flame. Turn them from time to time so that they cook evenly. In about 10 minutes, depending on the size of the aubergine, the skin will become crisp and the flesh will be cooked through. To test, drive a knife through the broadest part.

1 large aubergine
2 tablespoons sunflower oil
½ teaspoon cumin seeds
1 medium red onion, finely chopped
1 teaspoon ginger-garlic paste
   (see page 173)
1 fresh green chilli, finely chopped
2 tablespoons tomato purée
1 teaspoon turmeric powder
1 teaspoon ground coriander
salt, to taste
2 teaspoons roasted peanuts
handful fresh coriander leaves,
   washed and finely chopped
lemon wedge

preparation time 10 minutes
cooking time 30 minutes
serves 4

1. Either smoke the aubergine over a gas flame (see above) or brush it lightly with oil and place under a hot grill, turning it from time to time until soft.

2. Cool the aubergine slightly and then peel off the skin – it should come off easily. Place the flesh in a bowl and mash with a fork.

3. Heat the oil in a heavy-based saucepan and fry the cumin seeds over a high heat until they start to change colour. Add the onion and fry until soft – about 5 minutes.

4. Add the ginger-garlic paste and green chilli and fry for 1 minute. Add the tomato purée and spice powders and cook for a couple of minutes until well blended. Season with salt.

5. Stir in the mashed aubergine and peanuts, sprinkle with fresh coriander and serve with a wedge of lemon on the side.

LAL KOBICHI BHAJI 🔥🔥

red cabbage with mustard

Red cabbage gets its beautiful colour from flavonoids. These, along with vitamin C, make red cabbage a powerful antioxidant. The juice of red cabbage has been used to treat peptic ulcers for many years. In Ayurveda, red cabbage is classed as cold and heavy, making it difficult to digest – especially for people with a Vata constitution. People suffering from thyroid problems such as goitre should avoid it.

2 tablespoons sunflower oil
1 teaspoon black mustard seeds
½ teaspoon cumin seeds
large pinch asafoetida
2 green chillies, slit down the
    middle with the stalks left intact
300g red cabbage, finely chopped
salt, to taste
1 tablespoon lemon juice
3 tablespoons desiccated coconut

preparation time 10 minutes
cooking time 20 minutes
serves 4

1. Heat the oil in a heavy-based saucepan over a high heat and add the mustard seeds. As they pop, add the cumin and asafoetida. Stir in the chillies.

2. Add the red cabbage and salt. Pour in 3–4 tablespoons water and bring to a boil. Reduce the heat, cover and cook for 10 minutes, or until the cabbage is tender.

3. Take off the heat and stir in the lemon juice and coconut.

BHINDI KI SUBZI ☺ ☺ ☺

okra with coconut and kokum

Kokum is a tart, purple fruit which grows in western India. It is available in its dried, petal-shaped form from Indian grocers, and can be stored for a number of years. Ayurveda considers kokum to be healing for infections and skin-related problems.

When cooking okra, avoid adding any water to the pan because it will make the okra slimy. Combining it with acidic foods such as tomatoes, kokum or lemon juice will help to eliminate any natural slime.

2 tablespoons sunflower oil
1 teaspoon black mustard seeds
½ teaspoon cumin seeds
1 medium onion, finely sliced
300g okra, washed, dried, tops removed and flesh cut in half lengthways
1 teaspoon turmeric powder
½ teaspoon chilli powder
4 petals of kokum (available from Indian grocers)
salt, to taste
1 tablespoon lemon juice
2 tablespoons freshly grated coconut (or desiccated coconut)
small handful fresh coriander leaves, washed and finely chopped

preparation time 10 minutes
cooking time 30 minutes
serves 4

1. Heat the oil over a high heat in a kadhai or heavy-based saucepan and add the mustard seeds. When they pop, add the cumin seeds. As they darken, add the onions and fry until soft – about 5 minutes.

2. Add the okra and stir well.

3. Add the spice powders, kokum, salt and lemon juice and give everything a good stir to coat the okra in the oil and spices.

4. Cover and cook over a low heat, stirring frequently to keep it from sticking, until the okra is done – about 20 minutes. It will change from being slimy to feeling quite firm.

5. Stir in the coconut and fresh coriander and take off the heat.

GAJAR METHI

fenugreek leaves with carrot

1 bunch fresh fenugreek leaves
 (available from Indian grocers in
 conveniently tied bunches)
1 tablespoon sunflower oil
½ teaspoon cumin seeds
large pinch asafoetida
3 large carrots, washed and cut
 into 2cm cubes
¼ teaspoon chilli powder
½ teaspoon turmeric powder
1 teaspoon ground coriander
salt, to taste

preparation time 15 minutes
cooking time 25 minutes
serves 4

1. Pinch the leaves off the fenugreek, discarding the thick, central stalks. Wash, drain and roughly chop the leaves.

2. Heat the oil in a heavy-based saucepan and fry the cumin seeds over a high heat until they start to darken. Add the asafoetida and carrots, and then sprinkle in the powdered spices. Cook for 2–3 minutes, stirring carefully to prevent the spices from scorching.

3. Add the chopped fenugreek and salt. Stir-fry for 2–3 minutes until the leaves have wilted, and then pour in 3–4 tablespoons water. Cover and cook over a medium heat for 10–12 minutes until the carrots are done.

4. To finish, take off the lid and cook on a high heat until any water has evaporated.

KANDYACHA ZUNKA

spring onions with gram flour

6 tablespoons gram flour
2 tablespoons sunflower oil
1 teaspoon black mustard seeds
½ teaspoon cumin seeds
large pinch asafoetida
10 curry leaves
300g spring onions, finely chopped
½ teaspoon turmeric powder
1 teaspoon ground coriander
salt, to taste

preparation time 20 minutes
cooking time 20 minutes
serves 4

1. Place the gram flour in a heavy-based saucepan and dry-roast it over a low heat, stirring all the time to prevent it from scorching, until the aroma and colour change – this will take 7–8 minutes.

2. Meanwhile, heat the oil over a high heat in a clean pan. Add the mustard seeds, wait for them to crackle, and then add the cumin, asafoetida and curry leaves. Fry for 1 minute.

3. Add the spring onions, powdered spices and salt, and mix well to coat them in the oil and spices.

4. Reduce the heat and stir-fry the onions for 5 minutes until soft.

5. Stir in the roasted gram flour – it will absorb any liquid in the pan to form clumps. Break up the clumps to cook them. Take off the heat when the flour has absorbed all the liquid and turned golden brown.

PANEER SIMLA MIRCH

cottage cheese with mixed peppers

Peppers are a rich source of vitamin C, lycopene and beta-carotene. In Ayurveda, peppers are classed as sweet and warm, making them most suitable for people with a Kapha constitution. Some Vata people find them easier to digest when cooked. They can be slightly aggravating to Pitta because of their pungency.

2 tablespoons sunflower oil
1 teaspoon cumin seeds
300g mixed peppers (stalks and
  seeds removed), chopped
½ teaspoon turmeric powder
½ teaspoon chilli powder
½ teaspoon ground coriander
salt, to taste
150g paneer (see page 173), cut into
  2.5cm cubes
small handful fresh coriander
  leaves, washed and finely chopped

preparation time 15 minutes
cooking time 15 minutes
serves 4

1. Heat the oil in a heavy-based saucepan over a high heat. Add the cumin seeds and fry for a few seconds until they start to darken.

2. Add the peppers, powdered spices and salt and give everything a quick stir to coat the peppers in the oil and spices.

3. Add 3–4 tablespoons water and bring to the boil, and then reduce the heat, cover and cook for 5–6 minutes until the peppers are soft.

4. Fold in the paneer and let it soften for a minute, and then sprinkle in the fresh coriander. Serve hot or cold.

a child's lunchbox
cottage cheese with mixed peppers (PANEER SIMLA MIRCH)
wrapped in spiced multi-grain bread (THALIPEETH), page 33

BHARVA RINGNA

herby stuffed aubergines

Ayurveda describes coconut as cooling and sweet. However, it can cause problems for people with poor 'agni' or digestion. Coconut has laxative properties and its high fat content makes it unsuitable for people with high cholesterol.

75g freshly grated coconut
  (or desiccated coconut)
small handful fresh coriander
  leaves, washed and finely
  chopped
½ teaspoon chilli powder
1 teaspoon turmeric powder
salt, to taste
8 small aubergines (available
  from Indian grocers)
2 tablespoons sunflower oil
1 teaspoon black mustard seeds
1 teaspoon cumin seeds
8 new potatoes, pricked with a fork

preparation time 30 minutes
cooking time 30 minutes
serves 4

1. Combine the coconut, fresh coriander, chilli, turmeric and salt in a bowl.

2. Slit each aubergine lengthways into four, keeping the stem end intact so that the vegetable stays together. Fill the aubergines with the coconut mixture and place on one side.

3. Heat the oil in a heavy-based saucepan over a high heat and add the mustard seeds. Wait for them to pop, and then add the cumin seeds. Gently place the aubergines in the pan and arrange the potatoes in the gaps in between. Sprinkle any remaining stuffing over the top.

4. Add 100ml water to the pan and bring to the boil. Reduce the heat, cover and cook for 15 minutes until the aubergines and potatoes are tender. Test the aubergines by piercing them with a knife.

NAVALKOL MASALA

knol khol with spices

Knol khol or kohlrabi is an excellent source of potassium, which helps lower the risk of kidney stones. Look for pale-coloured knol khol with tender, flexible stems. If the stems are tough, it is likely that the flesh has overripened and become fibrous.

2 tablespoons sunflower oil
½ teaspoon cumin seeds
large pinch asafoetida
1 green chilli, finely chopped
1 teaspoon turmeric
½ teaspoon chilli powder
1 teaspoon ground coriander
300g knol khol (kohlrabi), peeled
  and cut into 2cm cubes
salt, to taste

preparation time 10 minutes
cooking time 25 minutes
serves 4

1. Heat the oil in a heavy-based saucepan over a high heat and add the cumin seeds. Allow them to darken, and then add the asafoetida and chilli.

2. Add the spice powders and knol khol, season with salt and give everything a good stir to coat the knol khol in the oil and spices.

3. Add 4–5 tablespoons water and bring to the boil. Reduce the heat, cover and cook for 12–15 minutes until the knol khol softens enough to mean that you can break it in half using the edge of a ladle.

TENDLI UPKARI

ivy gourds with coconut

Ivy gourds ('tendli' or 'tindora') are small gourds each the size of a little finger that have a taste similar to courgettes, but with a hint of sourness. They are available from Indian grocers, in both fresh as well as frozen forms. The best tindora are bright green and crisp. When they become stale, they turn crinkly and the insides go from pale green to orange.

2 tablespoons sunflower oil
½ teaspoon black mustard seeds
½ teaspoon cumin seeds
3 dried red chillies (seeds removed)
pinch of asafoetida
300g ivy gourd (tindora), sliced
   into 1cm discs
½ teaspoon turmeric powder
salt, to taste
2 tablespoons freshly grated coconut
   (or desiccated coconut)

preparation time 15 minutes
cooking time 25 minutes
serves 4

1. Heat the oil in a heavy, shallow saucepan and fry the mustard seeds over a high heat until they pop. Add the cumin seeds and allow them to darken slightly, and then add the chillies and asafoetida.

2. Add the tindora, turmeric and salt and give everything a good stir to coat the tindora in the oil and spices.

3. Add 2 tablespoons water, cover and bring to the boil. Reduce the heat and simmer until the tindora is tender but still retains a slight crunch – about 12–15 minutes.

4. Stir in the coconut and take off the heat.

spiced ridge gourd

Ridge gourds are very low in calories and carbohydrates, and they are therefore recommended for people with diabetes. To prepare them, simply peel away the ridges with a peeler – for older gourds, you might need to peel away the tough skin as well.

2 tablespoons sunflower oil
1 teaspoon cumin seeds
½ teaspoon aniseed
300g ridge gourd ('turia'), ridges peeled off and flesh cut into 2cm cubes
½ teaspoon turmeric powder
½ teaspoon chilli powder
salt, to taste

preparation time 15 minutes
cooking time 20 minutes
serves 4

1. Heat the oil in a heavy-based saucepan over a high heat and add the cumin seeds and aniseed. Just as they begin to change colour, add the ridge gourd and spice powders.

2. Give everything a good stir to coat the gourds in the oil and spices. Season with salt.

3. Add 2–3 tablespoons water and bring to the boil. Reduce the heat, cover and cook for 12–15 minutes until the gourds are just soft enough to break in half with the edge of a ladle.

KADHAI KARELA

stir-fried bitter gourd

Bitter gourd ('karela') is a dark green, knobbly vegetable with soft flesh and seeds, available from Indian grocers. It is quite an acquired taste and extremely bitter; however, soaking it in salted water for 15 minutes and then squeezing it dry will remove some of the bitterness. Karela is thought to lower blood sugar levels in those suffering from diabetes, and in India it is eaten to purify the blood.

2 tablespoons sunflower oil
1 teaspoon cumin seeds
1 medium onion, finely sliced
300g bitter gourd (karela), washed, thinly sliced and soaked in salted water for 15 minutes
2 ripe tomatoes, roughly chopped
1 teaspoon turmeric powder
½ teaspoon chilli powder
½ teaspoon garam masala
salt, to taste
1 tablespoon lemon juice
2–3 tablespoons finely chopped fresh coriander leaves, to garnish

preparation time 10 minutes (+15 minutes soaking time)
cooking time 30 minutes
serves 4

1. Heat the oil in a kadhai or heavy-based saucepan over a high heat. Add the cumin and allow it to darken slightly. Add the onions and fry until soft – about 5 minutes.

2. Add the slices of karela and stir-fry for 2–3 minutes to coat them in the hot oil and spices.

3. Add the tomatoes, spice powders, salt and lemon juice. Mix well.

4. Cook over a low heat, stirring frequently to keep it from sticking, until the karela is done – about 20 minutes.

5. Serve hot, sprinkled with chopped coriander leaves.

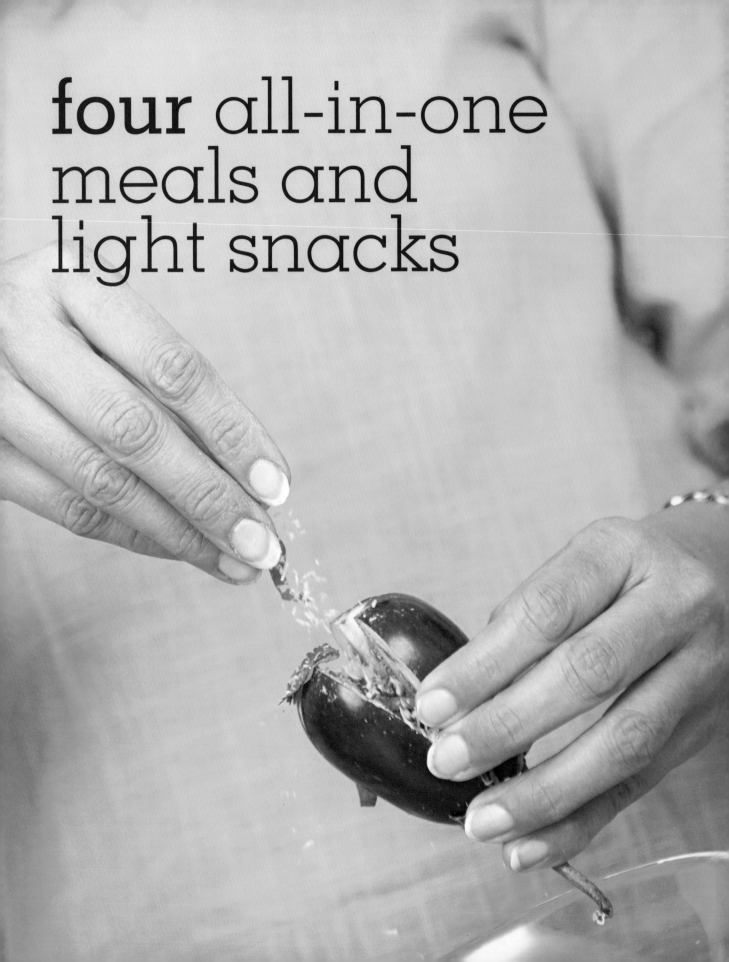

four all-in-one meals and light snacks

One thing that all Indians have in common is their passion for food. People find occasions to eat all through the day. Breakfast, elevenses or 'tiffin', lunch, tea and dinner are all important, as are all the snacky meals in between.

This is not to say that the cuisine or the snacks are unhealthy. On the contrary – much Indian food is very nutritious. In this chapter, I have included one-pot dishes that can be eaten as a complete meal and can be made very quickly. I find these recipes a great blessing when I return home after work with very little time left to cook, or if the family is not particularly hungry. We sometimes have them for breakfast or for tea, so they are quite versatile! Most can be eaten with yogurt and a side salad.

Ayurvedic wisdom

Small quantities of simple foods can bring 'agni' or the digestive fire back into balance. However, Ayurveda cautions against frequent snacking because this can create toxins in the body.

QUINOA UPMA

quinoa stir-fried with spices and vegetables

'Upma' is a light meal served for breakfast, for brunch or at teatime in southern India. It is traditionally made with semolina, although in this recipe I have used protein-rich quinoa. I quite like the contrast of flavours, colours and textures in this dish – the pearly crunchiness of the quinoa beautifully offsets the jewel-like vegetables and herbs.

300g quinoa
2 tablespoons sunflower oil
½ teaspoon black mustard seeds
½ teaspoon cumin seeds
2 small green chillies, slit in half lengthways with the stalks left intact
10 curry leaves
large pinch asafoetida
4 tablespoons frozen peas
1 carrot, finely diced
½ teaspoon turmeric powder
salt, to taste
small handful fresh coriander leaves, washed and finely chopped

preparation time 10 minutes (+ 5 minutes soaking time)
cooking time 25 minutes
serves 4

1. Place the quinoa in a bowl, cover with hot water and leave to soak for 5 minutes. This loosens the outer coating of saponin, which can give the quinoa a bitter taste. Rinse twice.

2. Heat the oil in a heavy-based saucepan over a high heat and add the mustard seeds. Wait for them to pop, and then add the cumin seeds and fry until slightly dark. Add the chillies, curry leaves and asafoetida.

3. Add the peas, carrots and turmeric and give them a quick stir to coat them in the oil and spices. Add the quinoa and salt.

4. Pour in 500ml hot water and bring to the boil. Reduce the heat and simmer, covered, for 20 minutes until the quinoa is cooked – it should be dry and translucent and will retain its crunchy texture.

5. Loosen the quinoa with a fork and sprinkle with fresh coriander. Serve hot or cold.

SABUDANA KHICHDI

spiced pearl sago

Sago is the starch extracted from the sago palm and it is sold as tiny 'pearls'. It is a popular snack food in India and is also used in a variety of desserts. Although sago has very little vitamin content, it is very high in carbohydrates – making it a real energy-booster. Here, I have combined it with peanuts, a high-protein food.

300g pearl sago (available from Indian grocers)
2 tablespoons sunflower oil
1 teaspoon black mustard seeds
1 teaspoon cumin seeds
2 green chillies, slit lengthways with the stalks left intact
12 curry leaves
salt, to taste
pinch of sugar
4 tablespoons roasted peanuts, roughly crushed
4 tablespoons freshly grated coconut (or desiccated coconut)
small handful fresh coriander leaves, washed and finely chopped
2 teaspoons lemon juice

preparation time 10 minutes (+ 20 minutes soaking time)
cooking time 20 minutes
serves 4

1. Place the sago in a bowl, cover with water and leave to soak for 20 minutes. Drain thoroughly.

2. Heat the oil in a heavy-based saucepan over a high heat and add the mustard seeds. When they pop, add the cumin, green chilli and curry leaves and fry together for 1 minute.

3. Reduce the heat and add the drained sago, stirring all the time to prevent lumps from forming.

4. Add the salt, sugar and peanuts and combine thoroughly. Cook on a very low heat, stirring all the time, until the sago is cooked – about 10 minutes. If the sago starts to stick to the bottom of the pan, add a little water and stir carefully.

5. Garnish with coconut and fresh coriander and sprinkle with lemon juice.

PANEER RAJMA KE SAMOSE 🌀

red bean and paneer samosa

Most people seem to love samosas; however, I cannot ever justify eating the deep-fried ones! Here is my recipe for baked samosas, using high-protein red kidney beans and creamy paneer for the filling. Serve hot or cold.

1 tablespoon sunflower oil,
   plus extra for brushing
½ teaspoon cumin seeds
½ teaspoon turmeric powder
1 teaspoon ground coriander
1 green chilli, very finely chopped
150g paneer (see page 173),
   cut into 1cm cubes
150g tinned red kidney beans,
   rinsed and drained
salt, to taste
500g ready-rolled filo pastry
   (or samosa strips)

preparation time 10 minutes
cooking time 40 minutes
makes 12

1. Preheat your oven to 220°C/425°F/gas mark 6. Heat 1 tablespoon oil in a heavy-based saucepan and fry the cumin seeds over a high heat for a few seconds until they start to darken. Reduce the heat.

2. Add the spice powders and chilli, followed immediately by the paneer and beans.

3. Season with salt and cook for 2–3 minutes, or until well blended. Leave to cool slightly.

4. Line a baking tray with aluminium foil.

5. Lay a sheet of pastry on a flat surface. Place a teaspoon of the bean and paneer mixture near the top left-hand corner. Lift the top left-hand corner over the filling to enclose it, making a triangle shape. Wrap up the samosa to form a neat triangular parcel and brush with oil. Make up the remaining samosas in the same way and arrange on the lined baking tray.

6. Bake in a hot oven for 20–25 minutes, turning once.

SINDHI KADHI

rice and vegetables in a gram flour stew

This dish is based on a traditional recipe from the Sindhi community, who immigrated to India from the region of Sind, now in Pakistan. I have incorporated a little brown rice into this version to make it a substantial meal in itself.

2 tablespoons sunflower oil
½ teaspoon fenugreek seeds
10 curry leaves
1 teaspoon finely grated fresh
   root ginger
600g mixed vegetables (e.g.
   aubergines, carrots, green beans,
   potatoes), cut into 1cm cubes
2 tablespoons gram flour, dry-
   roasted in a pan without any oil for
   7–8 minutes to intensify the flavour
1 x 400g tin chopped tomatoes,
   blitzed to a purée in a blender
3 teaspoons brown rice, washed
   and drained
salt, to taste

preparation time 15 minutes
cooking time 40 minutes
serves 4

1. Heat the oil in a heavy-based saucepan over a high heat and add the fenugreek seeds and curry leaves. Allow them to darken slightly, and then add the ginger.

2. Drop in the diced vegetables and give them a quick stir to coat them in the oil and spices.

3. Combine the dry-roasted gram flour with the puréed tomatoes and 300ml cold water.

4. Pour this mixture over the vegetables, sprinkle in the rice and season with salt.

5. Bring everything to the boil, and then reduce the heat, cover and cook for 30 minutes, stirring frequently, until the vegetables and rice are cooked.

KASTURI SEEKH KEBAB

lamb kebabs
with roasted vegetables

I find kebabs and barbecued meats very popular with most people, and they go really well with many vegetables. To make this dish more substantial, you could add some thickly sliced potatoes to the roasting pan – I usually par-boil them first to make them cook faster.

1 teaspoon chilli powder
1 teaspoon dried fenugreek leaves
   ('kasuri methi'), crushed
10 fresh mint leaves, finely chopped
1 teaspoon turmeric powder
1 teaspoon garam masala
2 teaspoons ginger-garlic paste
   (see page 173)
1 teaspoon ground cumin
salt, to taste
300g lean minced lamb
300g mixed vegetables (e.g. aubergine,
   peppers, butternut squash)
12 bamboo skewers
6–7 garlic cloves, peeled and sliced
sunflower oil, to drizzle

**preparation time 15 minutes
   (+ 20 minutes marinating time)
cooking time 15 minutes**
serves 4

1. Combine the chilli, fenugreek, mint, turmeric, garam masala, ginger-garlic paste and cumin in a large bowl. Season with salt and mix well together.

2. Add the minced lamb and knead well to blend the flavours. Cover with clingfilm and leave to marinate for 20 minutes.

3. Meanwhile, prepare the vegetables. Slice the aubergine and peppers and cut the squash into 1cm cubes, leaving the skin on. Preheat your oven to 220°C/425°F/gas mark 6.

4. Divide the lamb into 12 equal-sized balls. Wet your hands and shape the meat around the skewers to form sausage-shaped kebabs.

5. Line a baking tray with foil and place the kebabs on top. Surround with the vegetables, scattering them with sliced garlic. Drizzle with a little oil. Roast in the hot oven for 15 minutes until the meat is cooked and the vegetables are tender.

MUGACHI USAL

stir-fried mung sprouts

The process of sprouting creates a host of biochemical changes in which complex components break down into simpler substances that are easier to digest. Sprouted legumes have higher amounts of vitamin C, iron and calcium than those that are not sprouted.

150g dried green mung beans
1 tablespoon sunflower oil
½ teaspoon black mustard seeds
½ teaspoon cumin seeds
8 curry leaves
1 small green chilli, finely chopped
1 medium onion, finely chopped
½ teaspoon turmeric powder
salt, to taste
2 tablespoons desiccated coconut
1 tablespoon finely chopped fresh
    coriander leaves
1 tablespoon lemon juice

preparation time 10 minutes
    (+ 5 hours soaking time
    + overnight sprouting time)
cooking time 25 minutes
serves 4

1. Soak the mung beans in cold water for 5 hours, and then tie them in a piece of muslin and put them in a warm place, such as an airing cupboard, to sprout overnight.

2. The following day, wash the sprouted beans in cold water and drain in a colander.

3. Heat the oil in a heavy-based saucepan over a high heat and add the mustard seeds. Allow them to pop, and then add the cumin seeds, curry leaves and green chilli. Add the onion and fry for 3–4 minutes until soft.

4. Tip in the sprouted beans, turmeric and salt. Add 2–3 tablespoons water and cook over a medium heat for 10–12 minutes, or until the beans are tender but not mushy, adding more water if necessary.

5. Take off the heat and stir in the coconut, coriander and lemon juice. Serve warm or cold.

PULI SADHAM

tamarind and nut rice

This easy, all-in-one meal is packed with protein in the form of lentils, cashew nuts and peanuts.

300g brown basmati rice, washed and drained
2 tablespoons sunflower oil
½ teaspoon black mustard seeds
large pinch asafoetida
4 dried red chillies (seeds removed), crumbled
1 teaspoon split yellow gram lentils ('chana dal')
2 teaspoons cashew nuts
2 teaspoons peanuts
10 curry leaves
1 tablespoon tamarind paste, mixed with 6 tablespoons water
salt, to taste

preparation time 5 minutes
cooking time 30 minutes
serves 4

1. Place the rice in a saucepan with 800ml hot water and bring to the boil. Reduce the heat, stir, cover and simmer for 20 minutes until the rice is cooked.

2. Heat the oil in a heavy-based saucepan over a medium heat. Add the mustard seeds, asafoetida, chillies, lentils, cashew nuts, peanuts and curry leaves and fry together for 1 minute.

3. Stir in the tamarind and salt. Cook until the mixture is thick and the lentils are soft – about 8–9 minutes.

4. Fold in the cooked rice and serve hot.

a Diwali dinner

- tamarind and nut rice (PULI SADHAM)
- ivy gourds with coconut (TENDLI UPKARI), page 115
- green beans in a tomato curry (FARASBEAN BHAJI), page 93
- black lentils cooked with spices (KALI DAL), page 78
- pomegranate and yogurt raita (ANAAR KA RAITA), page 142
- bottle-gourd pudding (LAUKI KI KHEER), page 166

JAAE KI KHICHADI

spiced oat stew

This is a quick snack to eat at any time of the day. Oats are an excellent source of fibre and are also said to reduce high blood cholesterol levels. They have a low glycaemic index level, which means that the carbohydrates in them are absorbed into the blood slowly, keeping the blood sugar levels stable.

1 tablespoon sunflower oil
5 cloves
10 peppercorns
1 bay leaf
½ teaspoon cumin seeds
½ teaspoon turmeric powder
200g oats, washed and drained
4 tablespoons frozen peas
salt, to taste

preparation time 5 minutes
cooking time 10 minutes
serves 4

1. Heat the oil in a large, heavy-based saucepan over a high heat and fry the cloves, peppercorns, bay leaf, cumin seeds and turmeric for 1 minute.

2. Add the oats, peas and salt and give them a quick stir to coat them in the oil and spices.

3. Pour in 300ml hot water and bring to the boil. Reduce the heat and simmer for about 10 minutes, or until the oats are creamy. This dish should be quite moist, which increases its digestibility. If it is too dry, add a little more water. Serve with natural yogurt.

TIKHAT POHE

flaked rice with vegetables

I often make this dish for my family when they aren't feeling very hungry and they don't want a full-blown meal. Cumin is a slightly bitter spice, which makes it a good detoxifier. It is generally added to the hot oil at the start of cooking, releasing its aromatic, healing fragrance which goes on to flavour the whole dish.

300g Indian rice flakes (medium 'pawa'), available from Indian grocers
2 medium potatoes, cut into 2cm cubes
2 tablespoons fresh or frozen peas
1 teaspoon turmeric powder
salt, to taste
1 tablespoon sunflower oil
1 teaspoon black mustard seeds
½ teaspoon cumin seeds
large pinch asafoetida
2 fresh green chillies, very finely chopped
12 curry leaves
1 medium onion, finely chopped
2 teaspoons lemon juice
small handful fresh coriander leaves, washed and finely chopped
1 ripe tomato, finely chopped

preparation time 10 minutes
cooking time 25 minutes
serves 4

1. Soak the rice flakes in water for 5 minutes.

2. Place the potatoes and peas in a saucepan and cover with water. Bring to the boil, and then reduce the heat and simmer for 6–7 minutes until tender.

3. Drain the rice flakes and combine them in a bowl with the turmeric and salt.

4. Heat the oil in a heavy-based saucepan over a high heat and add the mustard seeds. Wait for them to pop, and then add the cumin, asafoetida, chillies and curry leaves. Add the onions and fry for 5 minutes until soft.

5. Drain the potatoes and peas and add them to the pan. Give them a quick stir to coat them in the oil and spices, and then tip in the flaked rice and combine thoroughly.

6. Reduce the heat and add 4 tablespoons water. Cover and cook for 7–8 minutes, or until the potatoes are slightly mushy and the dish is creamy in texture. Squeeze in the lemon juice.

7. Serve hot, garnished with fresh coriander and chopped tomatoes.

TANDOORI MURGH AUR ALOO

tandoori-style chicken and potatoes

This quick, all-in-one supper dish is cooked in the oven, leaving you with extra time to relax! I like to serve it with a mixed salad.

4 medium potatoes, thickly sliced
8 skinless chicken drumsticks
1 onion, finely sliced (to garnish)

FOR THE MARINADE:
1 tablespoon ginger-garlic paste
  (see page 173)
½ teaspoon chilli powder
½ teaspoon turmeric powder
½ teaspoon ground cumin
½ teaspoon ground coriander
1 teaspoon garam masala
2 tablespoons lemon juice
2 tablespoons sunflower oil
salt, to taste

preparation time 10 minutes
  (+ 15 minutes marinating time)
cooking time 30 minutes
serves 4

1. Line 2 baking trays with foil. To make the marinade, combine the ginger-garlic paste, ground spices, lemon juice, oil and salt in a large mixing bowl.

2. Dip the potato slices into the marinade and arrange them on one of the lined baking trays. Add the chicken drumsticks to the rest of the marinade and combine thoroughly. Leave to stand for 15 minutes.

3. Preheat your oven to 220°C/425°F/gas mark 6.

4. Arrange the marinated drumsticks on the remaining baking tray and cover with foil.

5. Bake the chicken and potatoes in the hot oven for 20–25 minutes, or until the chicken is cooked through and the potatoes are golden brown.

6. Garnish with sliced onions and serve immediately.

TAMATER PALAK KA SHORBA ⬣

tomato and spinach soup with paneer

I love this dish for its simplicity, ease and great nutritional value. The paneer adds protein, while the vegetables provide a host of nutrients such as lycopene and iron. The spices make it a lovely warming soup for winter, served with some crusty bread. In summer, you might like to leave out the garam masala.

1 tablespoon sunflower oil
4 handfuls fresh spinach, washed and roughly chopped
3 ripe tomatoes, roughly chopped
3 tablespoons split mung dal, washed and drained
¼ teaspoon garam masala
½ teaspoon finely grated fresh root ginger
½ teaspoon ground cumin
salt, to taste
small handful paneer (see page 173), cut into 1cm cubes

preparation time 10 minutes
cooking time 25 minutes
serves 4

1. Heat the oil in a heavy-based saucepan over a high heat. Add the spinach, tomatoes, mung dal, garam masala and ginger and stir for a few minutes. Pour in 600ml water and bring to the boil. Reduce the heat and simmer for about 10 minutes, or until the mung dal is cooked.

2. Cool the mixture slightly, and then liquidise in a blender to give a coarse purée, adding powdered cumin and salt to taste. Serve topped with cubes of paneer.

SOYA KI MISAL

spiced edamame beans

Edamame beans, also known as soya beans, are grown widely in many parts of India. They are available fresh or frozen in the West and they are an excellent source of high-quality protein. Edamame beans contain large amounts of all the essential amino acids, and they have been attributed with the ability to lower blood cholesterol.

2 tablespoons sunflower oil
½ teaspoon black mustard seeds
½ teaspoon cumin seeds
pinch of asafoetida
2 green chillies, finely chopped
1 small onion, finely chopped
1 red pepper (stalk and seeds
    removed), finely chopped
300g fresh or frozen edamame beans
    (soya beans)
½ teaspoon turmeric powder
1 teaspoon lemon juice
salt, to taste
4 tablespoons natural, low-fat yogurt
    (probiotic, if possible)
small handful fresh coriander leaves,
    washed and finely chopped
1 tablespoon raisins

preparation time 10 minutes
cooking time 25 minutes
serves 4

1. Heat the oil in a heavy-based saucepan over a high heat and fry the mustard seeds until they pop. Add the cumin seeds, asafoetida, chillies and onion. Fry for 5 minutes until the onion is soft, turning the heat down when the onion starts to turn brown.

2. Add the red pepper and edamame beans and stir to coat them in the oil and spices. Sprinkle in the turmeric, lemon juice and salt. Pour in 4–5 tablespoons water and bring to the boil.

3. Reduce the heat and simmer for 15–20 minutes until the beans are cooked.

4. Serve warm, topped with the yogurt, coriander and raisins.

a healthy packed lunch

- spiced edamame beans (SOYA KI MISAL)
- red bean and paneer samosa (PANEER RAJMA KE SAMOSE), page 122
- cucumber and mint raita (KHEERE PUDINA KA RAITA), page 136
- carrot and cashew salad with honey (GAJAR KA SALAAD), page 137

five salads
and raitas

Every Indian meal is accompanied by a fresh seasonal salad, which could mean a few sliced tomatoes or a more elaborate one with a specially made dressing. Salads are called by different names in India, depending on the ingredients or texture.

A salad that is dressed with yoghurt is usually a 'raita', whereas a finely cut salad is known as a 'kuchumber'. A raita cools down a meal, especially if it too spicy, although often a raita will itself include a spice or two such as cumin and pepper. In the south, a raita will sometimes be known as a 'pachadi'.

A kuchumber is variously called a 'kachoomer' or 'koshimbir' and is made of tiny, raw vegetables all mixed together (in Hindi, 'kacha' means raw). It may be dressed with seasoned lemon juice or vinegar, and the vegetables are finely diced to allow them to be eaten with a mouthful of rice or roti with curry, or with dry dishes such as kebabs.

ayurvedic wisdom

Most salads are considered cooling and are therefore recommended for Pitta. Yoghurt, which is one of the ingredients of a raita, initially has a cooling effect on the body but this gradually turns to warming.

KHEERE PUDINA KA RAITA

cucumber and mint raita

Cumin seeds that have been freshly toasted and then ground have a completely different aroma from the powdered cumin you can buy in shops.

½ cucumber, coarsely grated with the skin on
handful mint leaves, washed and finely chopped
200ml natural, low-fat yogurt
salt, to taste
½ teaspoon cumin seeds

preparation time 10 minutes
cooking time 2 minutes
serves 4

1. Combine the cucumber, mint, yogurt and salt in a serving bowl.

2. Heat a small saucepan and dry-roast the cumin seeds over a medium heat until they start to darken and release their aroma. Tip them into a mortar and crush to a fine powder. Sprinkle over the cucumber and yogurt and combine well.

MOOLI KA RAITA

white radish salad

Young mooli is creamy in colour and quite malleable. At this stage it is mild tasting and quite sweet; however, as it gets older, the skin hardens and the flesh becomes more pungent. Mooli is acceptable by Pitta and Kapha, but can aggravate Vata.

150g Indian white radish ('mooli'), coarsely grated
salt and pepper, to taste
1 teaspoon sunflower oil
½ teaspoon black mustard seeds
½ teaspoon cumin seeds
5 tablespoons natural, low-fat yogurt

preparation time 10 minutes
cooking time 5 minutes
serves 4

1. Combine the radish with the salt and pepper in a serving dish.

2. Heat the oil in a small pan and add the mustard and cumin seeds. Allow the mustard seeds to pop and wait for the cumin seeds to colour slightly. Pour the oil and spices over the radish mixture. Add the yogurt and mix lightly.

GAJAR KA SALAAD

carrot and cashew salad with honey

This salad is a great dish to take to the office as part of a healthy packed lunch. It can be prepared the night before and is full of energy-boosting cashew nuts and honey. Honey is cherished the world over for its healing properties, and it is an excellent ingredient to include in your diet when you are feeling run down or suffering from a sore throat.

1 teaspoon sunflower oil
½ teaspoon black mustard seeds
½ teaspoon cumin seeds
4 large carrots, washed and grated
2 tablespoons unsalted cashew nuts
salt, to taste
small handful fresh coriander leaves, washed
1 teaspoon runny honey

preparation time 5 minutes
cooking time 5 minutes
serves 4

1. Heat the oil in a small saucepan over a medium heat. When it is hot, add the mustard seeds and allow them to pop. Stir in the cumin seeds and turn off the heat.

2. Combine the grated carrots and cashew nuts in a serving bowl. Drizzle over the hot oil and seeds and mix well together. Season to taste with salt.

3. Stir in the fresh coriander and honey.

CHUKANDAR KA SALAAD

beetroot and onion salad with fennel

The sweetness of the beetroot in this salad is enhanced by the sweetness of the fennel and red onion, making this dish a great accompaniment to spicy curries. I always use plain, rather than pickled, beetroot for this salad.

150g cooked beetroot, cut into 1cm cubes
1 small red onion, finely chopped
1 teaspoon sunflower oil
½ teaspoon fennel seeds
salt and pepper, to taste

preparation time 10 minutes
cooking time 2 minutes
serves 4

1. Combine the beetroot and onion in a serving bowl.

2. Heat the oil in a small pan and fry the fennel seeds for 1 minute until they start to darken.

3. Pour the fennel seeds, along with the oil, over the beetroot and onion mixture. Season with salt and pepper and combine thoroughly.

SUVE KA KACHUMBER

onion, tomato and dill salad

Dill is a cooling, digestive herb which is acceptable to all the doshas. If you are making this salad in advance, avoid adding the salt until the last minute or it will cause the juices from the vegetables to leach out and make the salad soggy.

1 red onion, finely chopped
2 ripe tomatoes, finely chopped
handful dill leaves, finely chopped
salt and pepper, to taste

preparation time 10 minutes
cooking time nil
serves 4

Mix everything together and serve.

PALAK KA RAITA

spinach and garlic raita

Garlic has been celebrated as a miracle food for many hundreds of years. Raw garlic contains a sulphur compound called allicin which is known to kill bacteria. When garlic is cooked, it produces another compound (diallyl disulphide-oxide), which is thought to lower blood cholesterol.

150g spinach, washed and drained
150g natural, low-fat yogurt
1 garlic clove, peeled and
    finely grated
salt, to taste

preparation time 10 minutes
cooking time 5 minutes
serves 4

1. Roughly chop the spinach and place it in a pan over a medium heat. Cook the spinach for 3–4 minutes until it has wilted, stirring regularly to stop it from scorching. Tip it into a colander and leave it to cool – you can reserve the cooking liquid to use in another recipe!

2. Combine the yogurt with the grated garlic and salt in a serving dish. Stir in the cooled spinach and serve immediately. If you are preparing the raita in advance, leave out the salt until the last minute or it will cause the spinach juices to leach out and make the salad soggy.

PANEER MAKHANPHAL KA SALAAD

paneer and avocado salad

FOR THE DRESSING:
1 teaspoon lemon juice
salt, to taste
1cm piece fresh root ginger,
    scraped and grated
pinch of chilli powder

2 large avocado pears
150g paneer (see page 173),
    cut into 1cm cubes

preparation time 10 minutes
cooking time nil
serves 4

1. Combine the ingredients for the dressing in a small jug.

2. To prepare the avocados, first cut lengthways down the middle and ease out the large stone by twisting the two halves carefully and gently pulling them apart. Slice the flesh and combine it with the paneer in a serving dish.

3. Pour the dressing over the top and serve immediately.

broad beans with black salt and coriander

'Kala namak' (black salt) comes from the Himalayas, where it has been used for centuries as a cooking and finishing salt. Its aroma is similar to that of cooked eggs, but it seems to lift the flavour of salads and relishes. It is recommended for people with high blood pressure or those on low-salt diets, due to its low sodium

150g broad beans (hulled weight),
  fresh or frozen
Indian black salt (kala namak),
  to taste

FOR THE DRESSING:
1 bunch (2 good handfuls) fresh
  coriander, washed and
  roughly chopped
2 garlic cloves, peeled and
  finely chopped
2.5cm piece fresh root ginger, scraped
  and finely chopped
2 fresh green chillies, roughly
  chopped
good squeeze of lemon juice
handful pomegranate seeds

preparation time 10 minutes
cooking time 10 minutes
serves 4

1. Place the broad beans in a saucepan, cover with water and bring to the boil. Reduce the heat, cover with a lid and simmer for 10 minutes until cooked. Drain, tip into a serving dish and season with black salt. Leave to cool.

2. Meanwhile, place the coriander, garlic, ginger, chillies and lemon juice in a blender and blitz to a fine paste with a few tablespoons water.

3. Scoop the dressing over the cooled beans, scatter with the pomegranate seeds and mix well together.

ANAAR KA RAITA 🔥🔥

pomegranate and yogurt raita

Ayurveda stresses the importance of including a full range of 'rasas' in your daily diet for maximum health benefit – from sweet, spicy and sour flavours to salty, bitter and astringent ones. Pomegranates are both astringent and sweet, as well as being packed with antioxidants, vitamins A, C and E and iron – a real superfood!

1 large pomegranate
8 tablespoons natural, low-fat yogurt
pinch of Indian black salt (kala namak), available from Indian grocers
black pepper, to taste

preparation time 10 minutes
cooking time nil
serves 4

1. Cut the pomegranate in half and scoop out the small, edible seeds with a spoon. Discard the outer skin and pulp.

2. Combine the yogurt, black salt and pepper in a serving bowl and stir in the pomegranate seeds.

---

a light alfresco lunch

- pomegranate and yogurt raita (ANAAR KA RAITA)
- beetroot and onion salad with fennel (CHUKANDAR KA SALAAD), page 138
- broad beans with black salt and coriander (SEIM PHALLI KA CHAAT), page 141
- spiced multi-grain bread (THALIPEETH), page 33

DAHI BAINGAN BHARTA

aubergine salad with red onion and tomatoes

This is a simple but tasty salad to serve with a variety of meat or vegetarian curries. It also makes a wonderful dip for barbecues – I like to grill the aubergine, wrapped in foil, on the hot coals. If you are making the salad in advance, avoid adding the yogurt until the last minute or it will dry out.

1 large aubergine
1 tablespoon sunflower oil, plus
   extra for brushing
1 medium red onion, finely chopped
1 medium green chilli, finely
   chopped
2 ripe tomatoes, roughly chopped
1 tablespoon finely chopped
   fresh coriander leaves
salt, to taste
150ml natural, low-fat yogurt

preparation time 10 minutes
cooking time 25 minutes
serves 4

1. Brush the aubergine with oil and place it under a hot grill to roast. Turn from time to time until the skin is scorched and the flesh is soft.

2. Allow the aubergine to cool slightly, and then peel off the skin – it should come off easily.

3. Place the aubergine flesh in a bowl and mash with a fork.

4. Heat 1 tablespoon oil in a small, heavy-based saucepan and add the onion. Fry over a medium heat until soft, and then add the chilli, tomatoes and coriander leaves. Season with salt and cook until the tomatoes are soft and mushy.

5. Allow the mixture to cool, and then combine it with the mashed aubergine and yogurt. Serve at once.

CHANNA CHAAT

spiced chickpea salad

This refreshing summer salad is flavoured with fresh coriander and lemon juice. In Ayurveda, lemons are used to cleanse the body of 'ama' or toxins.

1 x 400g tin chickpeas,
    drained and rinsed
1 small onion, finely chopped
½ teaspoon ground black pepper
1 teaspoon lemon juice
salt, to taste
small handful fresh coriander
    leaves, washed and roughly
    chopped
lemon wedge, to garnish

preparation time 10 minutes
cooking time nil
serves 4

Combine all the ingredients in a bowl and garnish with the lemon wedge.

six chutneys and relishes

The word chutney comes from the Hindi 'chatna', which means to lick. Chutney must be high in taste and add a kick to the meal, so it is usually salty, sweet, bitter or hot – and therefore eaten in small quantities.

Many varieties of chutney or relish are traditionally served with an Indian meal – from mango chutney to the hot lime pickle that is popular in the West. These allow each diner to create their own personal taste and heat level, whether they require heat in the form of chilli pickle or sweetness from mango or papaya. Most pickles that are made at home in India are sun dried, although there is also a vast range of commercially made pickles as well.

Some ingredients seem to have no other purpose than to be puréed into chutney. One such ingredient is the ridged part of the ridge gourd known as 'turia'. In my childhood, my grandmother would peel the gourd and instead of discarding the spiky ridges would stir-fry them and mix them with spices and coconut to be whizzed into delicious chutney. I found that nothing was wasted.

Ayurvedic wisdom

Chutneys are usually more intensely spiced than the rest of the meal and tend to stimulate 'agni' or the digestive fire. Many relishes can be quite heating and they are therefore best eaten in small quantities.

flax-seed and garlic chutney

Flax seeds, and their oil, have been used in traditional Indian medicine for centuries. They range from cream to brown in colour and are available from most Indian grocers. As a child, I was given flax-seed tea to bring down a fever and to heal colds and coughs. This chutney is a home remedy for people with sugar imbalances and high cholesterol. It tastes wonderful as a side dish with rice and pancakes – I even use it in sandwiches!

3 tablespoons brown flax seeds (alsi)
8 curry leaves
1 dried red chilli, broken in half
   and seeds shaken out
2 garlic cloves, peeled and
   finely sliced
pinch of salt

preparation time 5 minutes
cooking time 2 minutes
serves 4

1. Heat a small frying pan and dry-roast the flax seeds over a medium heat – they will start jumping out of the pan, so have a lid handy! As soon as the seeds finish popping, turn off the heat and add the curry leaves and red chilli. Shake them about in the hot pan for a few seconds, and then add the garlic.

2. Transfer everything to a small blender or coffee mill with a pinch of salt and blitz to a coarse powder. Store in an airtight jar in the refrigerator and use within a week.

DHANIYE KI CHUTNEY

coriander and peanut chutney

1 bunch (2 good handfuls) fresh
   coriander, washed and roughly
   chopped
2.5cm piece fresh root ginger,
   scraped and finely chopped
2 fresh green chillies, roughly
   chopped
2 tablespoons roasted peanuts
salt, to taste
good squeeze of fresh lemon juice

preparation time 10 minutes
cooking time nil
serves 4

1. Place the coriander, ginger, chillies and peanuts in a blender and blitz to a fine paste with a few tablespoons water. Season with salt.

2. Squeeze in the lemon juice and mix well. The final texture should be thick and creamy. Serve as an accompaniment to samosas or bhajias or use as a sandwich spread.

MEETHI IMLI KI CHUTNEY

sweet tamarind and vegetable chutney

1 tablespoon grated jaggery
   (or soft brown sugar)
2 tablespoons tamarind paste,
   mixed with 8 tablespoons water
large pinch chilli powder
½ teaspoon ground cumin
pinch of Indian black salt ('kala namak')
1 small carrot, washed and
   coarsely grated
1 tablespoon finely grated cucumber

preparation time 10 minutes
cooking time 10 minutes
serves 4

1. Place the jaggery (or brown sugar) and tamarind in a small saucepan and bring to the boil. Simmer over a low heat until the mixture turns shiny and the jaggery is completely melted. If the mixture starts to get too dry and sticky, add more water, although the final consistency should be quite thick.

2. Add all the rest of the ingredients and simmer for 5 minutes.

3. Leave to cool and then serve at room temperature as a sweet accompaniment to spicy dishes or snacks.

PAPEETE KI CHUTNEY

sweet papaya chutney (opposite)

In Ayurveda, papayas are described as light and bitter, and they are beneficial for all the doshas when ripe. Papayas are helpful to the digestion.

150g ripe papaya
good squeeze of lemon juice
salt, to taste
1 teaspoon sunflower oil
1 teaspoon black mustard seeds
½ teaspoon garam masala

preparation time 10 minutes
cooking time 2 minutes
serves 4

1. To prepare the papaya, first cut it in half and scoop out and discard the small black seeds. Remove the skin with a peeler and mash the flesh.

2. Combine the papaya with the lemon juice and salt in a bowl.

3. Heat the oil in a small saucepan, add the mustard seeds and wait for them to pop. Take them off the heat and add the garam masala.

4. Stir in the mashed papaya with the oil and spices and mix well together. This chutney will keep, covered, for 1–2 days in the fridge.

LAHSUN DAHI KI CHUTNEY

hot garlic chutney

This is a typical coastal recipe from western India. It is also delicious served as a relish, without the yoghurt, sprinkled on hot buttered toast.

3 tablespoons desiccated coconut
salt, to taste
2 dried red chillies (seeds removed)
5 garlic cloves, peeled
½ teaspoon tamarind paste
4 tablespoons natural, low-fat
    yoghurt

preparation time 10 minutes
cooking time 5 minutes
serves 4

1. Heat a small saucepan and dry-roast the coconut over a medium heat until brown. Add the salt and red chillies and roast for 1 minute.

2. Take off the heat and add the garlic and tamarind. Transfer the mixture to a blender or coffee mill and blitz to a fairly fine paste.

3. Stir in the yoghurt and serve immediately. Alternatively, store it without adding the yoghurt for up to 2 weeks in the fridge.

HALDI KA ACHAR

fresh turmeric root relish

Turmeric is one of the healthiest spices used in Indian cooking. The root looks like ginger and it can be found in Asian food shops. Turmeric is a powerful natural antiseptic and antioxidant, and it is considered healing to the liver.

4 teaspoons finely chopped
   fresh turmeric root
1 teaspoon finely chopped
   fresh root ginger
1 small green chilli, very
   finely chopped
big squeeze of lemon juice
salt, to taste

preparation time 10 minutes
cooking time nil
serves 4

Place all the ingredients in an airtight jar and shake well to blend. Store for up to a week in the fridge.

SABE KI CHUTNEY

apple chutney

I have a wonderful apple tree in my garden that produces a delightful crop of cooking apples each year. I love making this chutney to go with a hot curry. Ayurveda says that apples are light, sweet and cooling and can help to remove toxins from the body. Raw apples are suitable for Kapha and Pitta, but Vata constitutions need to eat them cooked.

1 tablespoon sunflower oil
½ teaspoon black mustard seeds
½ teaspoon fennel seeds
½ teaspoon chilli powder
2 cooking apples, peeled and roughly
   chopped
2 dates, stoned and finely chopped
1 teaspoon finely grated fresh root
   ginger
1 tablespoon lemon juice
salt, to taste
1 teaspoon jaggery (or brown sugar)

preparation time 25 minutes
cooking time 15 minutes
serves 4

1. Heat the oil in a heavy-based saucepan over a medium heat and add the mustard seeds. Wait for them to pop, and then add the fennel seeds. As they darken, add the chilli powder and apples.

2. Stir in the dates and ginger and season with lemon juice, salt and jaggery (or sugar). Cook for 7–8 minutes, stirring occasionally. Cool and serve with any main meal.

a vegetarian celebration
- black lentils cooked with spices (KALI DAL), page 78
- spinach and sweetcorn curry (MAKKAI PALAK), page 89
- baked yeast bread (NAAN), page 26
- apple chutney (SABE KI CHUTNEY)

seven
drinks

Although many people in the West associate Indian food with beer or lassi, in actual fact neither is traditionally drunk with an Indian meal. Most people will drink just water to cleanse the palate from time to time so that each flavour in the food can be appreciated and enjoyed. Flavoured drinks are meant for other times of the day – for example, the teas in this chapter may be served for breakfast or as an after-dinner digestive drink.

Contrary to belief, if you bite into a chilli, it is not water that will take away the discomfort but yogurt. Capsaicin, the compound that makes chillies hot, is insoluble in water but can be neutralised by yogurt.

Ayurvedic wisdom

Ayurveda suggests sipping a drink in moderation during a meal. Drinking too much water at a meal dilutes the digestive juices and makes the digestion sluggish. Water at room temperature is best; iced drinks only put out the 'agni' or the digestive fire and inhibit digestion.

Ayurveda does not consider alcohol to be unhealthy. In fact, many recipes for herbal wines exist in classic Ayurvedic texts. However, anything in excess is harmful and Pitta, especially, should be careful about drinking too much alcohol.

HARI LASSI

yogurt drink with crushed curry leaves

Yogurt is heavy and moist and therefore best suited to Vata. It is a wonderful digestive – in fact, many Indian people finish their meal with a spoonful of yogurt. Its action when it is eaten is initially cooling, but it becomes warming over time.

½ teaspoon cumin seeds
8 curry leaves
handful fresh coriander leaves,
    washed and finely chopped
300ml water
300ml natural, low-fat yogurt
salt, to taste

preparation time 10 minutes
cooking time 2 minutes
serves 4

1. Heat a small frying pan and dry-roast the cumin seeds until they start to darken. Tip them into a mortar and crush to a fine powder.

2. Combine the curry leaves and fresh coriander in a blender and blitz to a paste with 150ml water.

3. Once the herbs are finely blended, add the rest of the water, the yogurt and the salt. Blitz for a few more seconds to ensure everything is thoroughly combined.

4. Pour into glasses and sprinkle with the roasted cumin powder.

AAM KI LASSI

mango lassi

Ripe mangoes are balancing to all the doshas and they contain high amounts of vitamins A and C, which tone the tissues and build immunity. They are heating and can upset the digestion if eaten in excess. Choose ripe mangoes for this recipe, making sure there is some 'give' when they are squeezed gently.

2 ripe Indian mangoes (Alphonso or Kesar), stones removed
pinch of powdered cardamom
300g natural, low-fat yogurt (probiotic, if possible)
sugar, to taste
300ml water

preparation time 15 minutes
cooking time nil
serves 4

Peel and chop the mangoes and purée them in a blender. Mix with the other ingredients and dilute with the water to give a pouring consistency.

NIMBOO PANI

fresh lemonade with ginger

The hot summers of India have created the need for many cooling drinks such as this one. Keep a jug of this refreshing lemonade in the fridge during summer. You can also add summer fruit, such as berries and nectarines, for a delicious variation.

juice of 2 lemons
salt, to taste
honey, to taste
2.5cm piece fresh root ginger, scraped and finely grated
a few mint leaves, to garnish

preparation time 10 minutes
cooking time nil
serves 4

1. Combine the lemon juice, salt, honey and ginger in a jug and mix well.

2. Divide between 4 tall glasses and top up with cold water. Garnish with mint leaves.

JALJEERA

cumin seed cooler

This drink is usually served as a pre-dinner appetiser. You can adjust the seasoning to your taste, although the final drink should be a mixture of sweet, salty and spicy.

2 teaspoons cumin seeds
1 tablespoon tamarind paste,
    mixed with 6 tablespoons water
600ml water
2 tablespoons grated jaggery
½ teaspoon Indian black salt
    ('kala namak')
4 tablespoons finely chopped fresh
    coriander leaves

preparation time 5 minutes
cooking time 2 minutes
serves 4

1. Dry-roast the cumin seeds in a small saucepan for a minute or so, until they start to darken. Tip them into a mortar and crush them to a fine powder.

2. Combine the tamarind, water, jaggery and black salt in a jug, stirring constantly until the jaggery has dissolved. Stir in the ground cumin and fresh coriander.

KASHAYA

flax-seed tea

Whenever I had a cold or a temperature as a child, my grandmother would make me this lovely tea. It instantly made me feel better and today I give it to my own children. The spices soothe the organs; the warmth restores the equilibrium.

1 teaspoon flax seeds
3 black peppercorns, crushed
2 cardamom pods, bruised
3 cloves, bruised
1cm piece fresh root ginger,
   scraped and sliced
600ml water
jaggery (or raw cane sugar), to taste

preparation time 2 minutes
cooking time 10 minutes
serves 4

1. Put the flax seeds in a saucepan and heat them with a lid on – this is to stop them jumping out of the pan when they get hot. When they have finished popping, add the spices, ginger and water and bring to the boil. Reduce the heat and simmer for 5 minutes.

2. Strain, and then stir in the jaggery (or sugar). Serve hot.

MASALA CHAI

spiced digestive tea

This is a wonderful after-dinner digestive. Cardamom helps lighten the effects of a heavy meal and settles the stomach; coriander seeds tone the digestive system.

1 teaspoon fennel seeds
3 cardamom pods, bruised
600ml water
3 teabags
honey, to taste
dash of milk (optional)

preparation time 1 minute
cooking time 10 minutes
serves 4

1. Place the spices in a heavy-based pan and dry-roast over a high heat for a minute or so until they start to sizzle and change colour.

2. Pour in the water and bring to the boil. Reduce the heat and simmer for 5 minutes. Add the tea bags and bring to the boil.

3. Take off the heat, strain and discard the spices and tea bags.

4. Sweeten to taste with honey and add a dash of milk, if desired.

HALDI KI CHAI

turmeric and jaggery tea

My good friend Gope gave me this recipe as a magic drink that could cure anything. I have been drinking this tea, once a day, for a while now – sometimes even without the jaggery – and I have experienced its good effects. It has helped my digestion, cleansed my system so that my skin glows and kept colds and coughs at bay.

600ml water
pinch of turmeric powder
few shavings of jaggery (about
  ½ teaspoon per mug)

preparation time 2 minutes
cooking time nil
Serves 4

1. Heat the water in a kettle.

2. Put a pinch of turmeric and some jaggery into 4 mugs and pour the boiling water over.

eight desserts

Every festival in India, and there are many, is associated with sweets and desserts. Sweets are offered to the gods as 'holy foods' and, as such, most are rich and heavy. Of course, India also has a great variety of tropical fruit, which means that a healthy pudding is always available.

Fruit is classed as cleansing by Ayurveda because it rids the body of toxins and is very easy to digest. Only fruit that has ripened naturally and is free from chemicals is considered to be truly healthy, so look for organically grown fruits or grow your own to make sure that you are not eating a load of chemicals as well.

Ayurvedic wisdom

Ayurveda cautions against eating too many sweet foods and does not recommend eating heavy desserts after a meal. This is because they sit on top of everything else in the stomach and are last in line to be digested. For maximum benefit, fruit should be eaten on its own or before a meal.

KHAJUR AUR BADAM KA HALWA

date and almond fudge

Indian halwa is quite rich and can be made of milk, vegetables (such as carrots), fruit (such as figs and dates) or nuts. Traditional Indian sweets ('mithai') are made with lots of ghee and sugar, but my version of halwa contains neither. Dates are a low-calorie, nutritionally rich food. Their selenium content lowers the risk of heart disease and cancer and, in traditional medicine, dates are even said to relieve a sore throat.

12 soft dates (stones removed) – choose plump varieties such as Medjool or Khadrawi (if using drier varieties such as Deglet Noor, poach in water for 5 minutes and drain or steam for 2–3 minutes until soft)
4 tablespoons orange juice
50g flaked almonds
2 tablespoons pumpkin seeds
large pinch finely crushed cardamom seeds (taken from 6 pods)
2 teaspoons ground almonds

preparation time 10 minutes
cooking time nil
makes 12 pieces

1. Place the dates in a bowl and mash them with a fork, adding orange juice to make a thick, rich pulp.

2. Fold in the flaked almonds, pumpkin seeds and cardamom.

3. Spread the ground almonds on a flat dish. Shape the date mixture with your hands into 12 cherry-sized balls and roll in the almonds. The halwa will keep for 3 days in the refrigerator.

SANTRE KA SHEERA

orange and semolina pudding with saffron

Oranges are known to purify the blood, stimulate 'agni' and tone the liver. Their long-term effects are sweet and cooling, making them most suited to Vata. Oranges are a great source of vitamin C, a water-soluble antioxidant that helps to boost immunity.

2 tablespoons sunflower oil
150g semolina
3 tablespoons brown sugar
2 sweet oranges, peeled and cut into
   segments with the pith removed
large pinch saffron
450ml hot water

preparation time 10 minutes
cooking time 20 minutes
serves 4

1. Heat the oil in a saucepan and fry the semolina for 5 minutes over a high heat until fragrant. Reduce the heat and add the sugar. Stir for 3–4 minutes until it has melted.

2. Add the oranges and saffron. Pour in 450ml hot water and stir to combine. Cover with a lid and cook over a low heat until the semolina is cooked and the mixture is dry and fluffy – about 6–7 minutes. Serve hot or cold.

a quick supper

- plain boiled rice (CHAVAL), page 18
- black-eyed beans with tuna (LOBHIA AUR MACCHI), page 60
- spiced ridge gourd (TURIA KI SABZI), page 116
- orange and semolina pudding with saffron (SANTRE KA SHEERA)

LAUKI KI KHEER

bottle gourd pudding

This unusual sounding dessert is actually quite popular in many parts of India. Bottle gourd is relatively cheap and also highly nutritious. You can substitute it with grated carrots if you wish.

1 medium bottle gourd ('doodhi'), peeled and cut into tiny cubes
300ml milk
2 tablespoons grated jaggery (or brown sugar)
½ teaspoon finely crushed cardamom seeds (taken from 6 pods)
2 teaspoons pumpkin or melon seeds

preparation time 10 minutes
cooking time 20 minutes
serves 4

1. Place the bottle gourd and milk in a saucepan and bring to the boil. Reduce the heat and simmer for 10–12 minutes until soft and translucent. There should still be some liquid left in the pan.

2. Add the jaggery and stir for 3–4 minutes until it has melted and blended into the milk – the jaggery will thicken the milk.

3. Take off the heat and add the cardamom powder. Mix well.

4. Cool, spoon into dishes and serve sprinkled with pumpkin or melon seeds.

MADGANE

lentil pudding with jaggery

This traditional pudding from southern India is typically made on festive days. I like it because, although it is filling, it is not rich or heavy and it is very healthy tasting. I remember eating it during my childhood, for the Ganesh festival that falls during the monsoon each year.

3 tablespoons broken basmati rice (this gives a better, sticky texture to the pudding than ordinary basmati rice)

4 tablespoons split yellow gram lentils ('chana dal'), washed and drained

4 tablespoons cashew nuts

2 tablespoons raisins

2 tablespoons freshly grated coconut (or desiccated coconut)

½ teaspoon finely crushed cardamom seeds (taken from 5–6 pods)

2 tablespoons jaggery (or brown sugar)

preparation time 10 minutes
cooking time 45 minutes
serves 4

1. Soak the rice in a little water while you prepare the rest of the ingredients.

2. Heat a small pan and dry-roast the lentils for 3–4 minutes until they start to change colour.

3. Take the lentils off the heat and transfer them to a bigger saucepan with the cashew nuts and raisins. Pour in 150ml water and bring to the boil. Reduce the heat and simmer for 30 minutes until the lentils are soft.

4. Meanwhile, drain the rice and blitz it in a blender with the coconut and cardamom powder, adding a few tablespoons water to get a smooth paste.

5. Scoop the rice and coconut paste into the cooked lentils and top up with enough water to give a pouring consistency. Add the jaggery (or brown sugar).

6. Cook on a low heat for 5 minutes until the rice is cooked. The final dish should be creamy and the consistency of thin custard.

MAKHANPHAL KA RASAYAN

avocado and sweet turmeric pudding

I have based this dish on a traditional recipe that is made with fruit and coconut milk. Avocados are high in monounsaturated fats and omega-3 fatty acids, both of which help to reduce blood cholesterol. They have the highest fibre content of all the fruits and are also very high in potassium. Although turmeric is not generally added to Indian sweets, I love the golden colour and health benefits it brings to the dish.

300ml unsweetened soya milk (or
   semi-skimmed milk, if you prefer)
large pinch turmeric powder
2 tablespoons grated jaggery
   (or brown sugar)
2 tablespoons cashew nuts
½ teaspoon finely crushed cardamom
   seeds (taken from 6 pods)
2 ripe avocados (stones removed),
   peeled and roughly chopped
1 tablespoon pomegranate seeds
   (or any red fruit, such as
   strawberries, cherries or
   cranberries), to garnish

preparation time 10 minutes
cooking time 5 minutes
serves 4

1. Place the soya milk, turmeric, jaggery (or sugar), cashew nuts and cardamom in a saucepan and bring to the boil, stirring all the time to dissolve the jaggery.

2. Take off the heat and cool completely. Stir in the avocado and serve topped with the pomegranate seeds.

---

summer lunch with friends
- meatballs in a fennel and ginger curry (MASALE KE KOFTE), page 43
- plain boiled rice (CHAVAL), page 18
- onion, tomato and dill salad (SUVE KA KACHUMBER), page 138
- avocado and sweet turmeric pudding (MAKHANPHAL KA RASAYAN)

LAPSI KHEER

cracked wheat and banana pudding

Ripe bananas are cooling, heavy and sweet, although their long-term effect is sour – making them fairly unsuitable for Kapha and Pitta if eaten in excess. They are good for heartburn, gas and inflammations of the gastro-intestinal tract.

Cracked wheat ('lapsi') is like couscous but slightly darker in colour, with slightly bigger grains. Wheat is a heavy grain and needs to be combined with moist foods to be properly digested.

150g cracked wheat ('lapsi')
4 tablespoons grated jaggery
   (or brown sugar)
150ml coconut milk
½ teaspoon finely crushed cardamom
   seeds (taken from 6 pods)
2 bananas, sliced

preparation time nil
cooking time 20 minutes
serves 4

1. Place the cracked wheat in a saucepan, cover with 300ml water and cook for 15 minutes until soft.

2. Stir in the jaggery and cook for 3–4 minutes until it has melted. Take off the heat.

3. Add the coconut milk and cardamom powder.

4. Fold in the sliced bananas and serve warm.

MODAK

steamed rice and coconut parcels

This festive dish is made on special occasions and it is a great treat for everyone. It requires a bit of patience because folding the parcels is quite a skilful process. If you are too quick, the rice pastry will tear. The best way to avoid this is to keep the dough moist by wetting your palms frequently.

1 tablespoon sunflower oil
220g rice flour
3 tablespoons grated jaggery
  (or brown sugar)
150g freshly grated coconut
  (or desiccated coconut)
½ teaspoon finely crushed
  cardamom seeds (taken from
  6 pods)

preparation time 10 minutes
cooking time 30 minutes
serves 4

1. Place 300ml water in a saucepan with the oil and bring to the boil. Reduce the heat and beat in the rice flour with a wooden spoon until it forms a ball of dough.

2. Take off the heat and cool slightly, and then knead to a soft, pliable dough.

3. Place the jaggery (or sugar) in a heavy-based saucepan and stir for 3–4 minutes over a low heat until it has melted. Add the coconut and cardamom and stir to combine.

4. Divide the rice dough into 15 balls each the size of a small plum.

5. Wet your palms with water and take a ball of dough in your palm. Flatten it into a disc. Place a portion of the coconut mixture in the middle and fold up the edges of the disc to join in a point on the top. The parcel should resemble a large teardrop. Seal the top well. If any cracks appear while you are folding up the parcel, seal by smoothing down with water.

6. Line a steamer with greaseproof paper and steam the parcels for 10–15 minutes until the casings have turned slightly translucent. Any leftover stuffing makes a great filling for pancakes!

the Indian store cupboard

spices

If you walk into an Indian spice shop, you will see shelves upon shelves of colourful fragrant spices, and it is easy to believe that every Indian home must have a great store of them. In actual fact, I tend to use about seven spices on a regular basis and these take me through most of my cooking – turmeric powder, chilli powder, ground cumin, ground coriander (seeds), cumin seeds, black mustard seeds and garam masala. When I refer to a powdered or ground spice, it means the spice that is available commercially in ground form.

Each spice used in Indian cooking has healing properties. Turmeric is a great antiseptic, cumin aids the digestion and chilli helps to regulate body temperature. Spices are available as seeds as well as powders and it is important to store them properly to get the best out of them. The way to do this is to keep them in a dark, dry container for no longer than 6 months. After this they will not become toxic, but they will certainly lose some of their flavour.

asafoetida ('hing')

Although it is native to Afghanistan, asafoetida has for ages been an essential part of Indian cookery and medicine. Because of its offensive smell, it is sometimes referred to as 'devil's dung'.

Asafoetida is the dried latex from the rhizomes of several species of ferula or giant fennel. It is the product of a tall, smelly, perennial herb, with strong, carrot-shaped roots. In March or April, just before flowering, the stalks are cut close to the root. A milky liquid oozes out, which dries to form asafoetida. This is collected and a fresh cut is made. This procedure continues for about 3 months from the first incision, by which time the plant has yielded up to 1kg of resin and the root has dried up.

Fresh asafoetida is whitish and solid and gradually turns pink to reddish-brown on exposure to oxygen. It is ochre coloured when sold commercially, and the most widely used form is a fine yellow powder or granules. Asafoetida has a pungent, unpleasant smell – quite like that of pickled eggs – due to the presence of sulphur compounds. On its own it is distasteful, but when it is added to Indian savouries it can complete the flavour of the dish.

Asafoetida keeps well for up to a year. Its powerful aroma complements lentils, vegetables and pickles. It is always used in small quantities – a tiny pinch added to hot oil before the other ingredients is enough to flavour a dish for 4.

fenugreek ('methi')

Ancient herbalists discovered that fenugreek aids digestion and the seeds are still eaten today to relieve flatulence, chronic cough and diarrhoea. Fenugreek is available in two forms – either as seeds or as leaves (either fresh or dried). The seeds are small, hard, oblong and ochre in colour. They are available whole, crushed or powdered and are known for their curry-like aroma and lingering taste. Fenugreek leaves ('kasuri methi') add a wholesome touch to meat, vegetable and onion-based curries. They are available in bundles and the tough stalks need to be discarded before use. Dried leaves and seeds should be stored in airtight jars to preserve their flavour. Use seeds within 6 months, dried leaves within 4 months.

jaggery

During the manufacture of sugar from sugar cane, as the cane turns to crystal, several by-products are formed: molasses, alcohol and jaggery. Jaggery is dehydrated sugar cane juice that hasn't been purified and therefore preserves all the qualities of the juice itself. In India, it is mostly produced by small cultivators using huge crushers powered by bullocks. Jaggery is as important in Indian cookery as sugar is in the West. It has a special flavour that cannot really be substituted with sugar, although brown or demerara sugar is the closest equivalent.

Jaggery ranges from mustard yellow to deep amber in colour, depending on the quality of the sugar cane juice. It is sticky, but crumbles easily. It has a heavy, caramel-like aroma that is slightly alcoholic – rather like sweet sherry or port – and a sweet, musky taste.
You can buy jaggery in various sizes, wrapped in plastic or jute cloth, from most Indian grocers. Use within 6 months.

basic recipes

ginger-garlic paste

Ginger and garlic are almost always used together in Indian cooking. To make ginger-garlic paste, you will need one part fresh root ginger to one and a half parts garlic. Never peel ginger because the medicinal part lies just beneath the skin – simply scrape it gently with a knife. Peel and roughly chop the garlic cloves and combine them with the ginger in a blender. Blitz to make a smooth puree with a few tablespoons of water.

I usually make this paste in big batches and freeze it in thin sheets between plastic. I also always have a jar of it in my fridge. This lasts up to a month and is extremely handy when I want to save time.

garam masala

Every Indian household has its own recipe for garam masala, although most people now find that commercially bought garam masala works just as well. Here is a recipe:

1 teaspoon black peppercorns
2 teaspoons cumin seeds
2cm cinnamon stick
1 teaspoon cardamom seeds
   (removed from 10–12 pods)
1 teaspoon cloves
3 bay leaves

Place the spices in a small saucepan and dry-roast them over a medium heat with no oil until they start to darken and release their fragrance - about 3–4 minutes. Tip them into a coffee mill and blitz them to a powder, or grind them by hand using a pestle and mortar. Store in an airtight jar and use within 6 months.

paneer

Paneer or Indian curd cheese is available in most Indian grocers, however it is also easy to make your own at home. To make 150g paneer, you will need:

450ml whole milk
2 tablespoons fresh lemon juice
   (or as much as it takes to curdle the milk)

Place the milk in a heavy-based saucepan and bring to the boil. Remove from the heat and add the lemon juice, stirring constantly until the milk separates into paneer (curds) and whey. Let it stand for a few minutes to coagulate completely, then strain through a piece of muslin or a very fine strainer. (Reserve the whey to use in doughs instead of water.) Place the paneer on a plate and weigh it down with a heavy object such as a pan until all the excess whey has drained out and the paneer is set. Cut and use as required. Any leftover paneer can be stored in the fridge for 3–4 days. Simply cover with fresh water to prevent it from drying out, replacing the water on a daily basis.

index